FINGERPRINTS

Titles in the True Forensic Crime Stories series:

BONES
DEAD PEOPLE DO TELL TALES
Library Ed. ISBN 978-0-7660-3669-7
Paperback ISBN 978-1-59845-363-8

CYBERCRIME
DATA TRAILS DO TELL TALES
Library Ed. ISBN 978-0-7660-3668-0
Paperback ISBN 978-1-59845-361-4

DNA AND BLOOD
DEAD PEOPLE DO TELL TALES
Library Ed. ISBN 978-0-7660-3667-3
Paperback ISBN 978-1-59845-362-1

FINGERPRINTS
DEAD PEOPLE DO TELL TALES
Library Ed. ISBN 978-0-7660-3689-5
Paperback ISBN 978-1-59845-364-5

GUN CRIMES
DEAD PEOPLE DO TELL TALES
Library Ed. ISBN 978-0-7660-3763-2
Paperback ISBN 978-1-59845-365-2

TRACE EVIDENCE
DEAD PEOPLE DO TELL TALES
Library Ed. ISBN 978-0-7660-3664-2
Paperback ISBN 978-1-59845-366-9

FINGERPRINTS

Dead People DO Tell tales

TRUE forensic CRIME stories

Chana Stiefel

Enslow Publishers, Inc.
40 Industrial Road
Box 398
Berkeley Heights, NJ 07922
USA
http://www.enslow.com

Library of Congress Cataloging-in-Publication Data

Stiefel, Chana, 1968–
Fingerprints : dead people do tell tales / Chana Stiefel.
p. cm. — (True forensic crime stories)
Includes bibliographical references and index.
Summary: "Uses true crime stories to explain the science of forensics and fingerprint evidence"
—Provided by publisher.
ISBN 978-0-7660-3689-5
1. Fingerprints—Juvenile literature. 2. Criminal investigation—Juvenile literature. 3. Forensic sciences
—Juvenile literature. I. Title.
HV6074.S75 2010
363.25'8—dc22
2010001116

Paperback ISBN 978-1-59845-364-5

Printed in China

052011 Leo Paper Group, Heshan City, Guangdong, China

10 9 8 7 6 5 4 3 2 1

To Our Readers: We have done our best to make sure all Internet Addresses in this book were active and appropriate when we went to press. However, the author and the publisher have no control over and assume no liability for the material available on those Internet sites or on other Web sites they may link to. Any comments or suggestions can be sent by e-mail to comments@enslow.com or to the address on the back cover.

Photo Credits: Alex Garcia/Chicago Tribune/Newscom, p. 77; Alfred Pasieka/Photo Researchers, Inc., p. 18; The Art Archive/Alfredo Dagli Orti, p. 16; © 1999, Artville, LLC, p. 50 (map); Associated Press, pp. 6 (bottom), 31, 34, 50 (photo), 72, 75, 81, 89; Dennis Brack/Landov, p. 44; Dr. Richard Kessel & Dr. Randy Kardon/Tissues & Organs/Visuals Unlimited, Inc., p. 19; FBI, p. 30; Jim Varney/Photo Researchers, Inc., p. 61; Kathy Kmonicek/MCT/Landov, p. 38; Kevin Dietsch/UPI /Landov, p. 32; Library of Congress, pp. 8, 12; National Library of Medicine, p. 11; Patrick Landmann/Photo Researchers, Inc., p. 70; Philippe Psaila/Photo Researchers, Inc., p. 41; Reuters/Landov, p. 36; Robert Galbraith/Reuters/Landov, p. 60; Sheila Terry/Photo Researchers, Inc., p. 25; Shutterstock.com, pp. 1, 2, 3, 5 (background), 6 (top, background), 14, 16 (background), 20 (background), 22, 28 (background), 29, 33 (background), 35 (background), 46–47 (background), 48, 58, 68, 83 (background), 84–85 (background); The Star-Ledger, pp. 55, 56; ©Universal/Courtesy Everett Collection, p. 63; U.S. Army photo by Spc. David M. Sharp, p. 86; U.S. Customs and Border Protection, pp. 67, 91.

Cover Photo: Shutterstock.com

Contents

Check it out! Using a magnifying glass, compare the ridge patterns on the pads of your fingers to those of your friends and family. You might find some similarities, but did you notice that no two fingerprints are exactly the same?

INTRODUCTION

LEAVING A TRAIL

Have you ever thought about what makes you unique? Is it your looks? Your talent? Without a doubt, your one-of-a-kind personality makes you special. Yet it might surprise you that the one trait that makes you different from the other 6.9 billion people on the planet is right at the tips of your fingers. It's your fingerprints! Amazingly, no two people in the world—not even identical twins—have been found to share the same fingerprints.

If you look closely at your fingertips, you will notice tiny ridges, raised lines of skin that form interesting patterns. The wide variety of ways that these patterns swirl and whirl makes your fingerprints unique.

Because every person's prints are different, fingerprints have become essential clues in identifying criminals and solving crimes. Police have been comparing fingerprints to nab criminals for more than a century. Matching a suspect's fingerprints to those found at a crime scene has developed as both an art and a science. In the past, detectives spent months comparing prints lifted from a crime scene to suspects' prints filed on note cards. Today, computers narrow down the search and can help find a potential match in minutes. Fingerprint experts compare the prints closely and make the final call.

Since the early 1900s, fingerprints have helped solve millions of crimes. Recently, however, this technique is being questioned. Critics of fingerprint analysis are questioning whether the process is as foolproof as it seems. For example, how likely is it that two fingerprints from two different people are similar enough to confuse a fingerprint expert? The jury is still out. To learn more about fascinating fingerprints, the latest techniques to uncover them, how they are used to solve crimes, and the controversy surrounding them, read on!

Federal Penitentiary, Leavenworth, Kansas

1 The Wild Will West Story

What are fingerprints and what makes them unique?

On May 1, 1903, police brought a convicted criminal named Will West to the federal prison in Leavenworth, Kansas. When West arrived, the guards were certain they recognized him. However, West insisted that he had never been a prisoner there. Keep in mind that this happened long before police could run a computer check. The guards searched their files for "William West." Sure enough, they found another inmate by the same name who was currently at Leavenworth Prison. He was serving a life sentence for murder. This William West looked remarkably similar to the other Will West who had just arrived. Was this some kind of trick? What was going on?

BODY ID

IN THE EARLY 1800s, law enforcement officials had very unsophisticated ways of identifying criminals. Often, police officers with photographic memories would visit jails to see if they recognized prisoners. Or they would try to memorize faces in case inmates tried to commit other crimes after their release. Of course, this system was very flawed. People's appearances change over time. Memory is imperfect and unreliable. In addition, criminals could simply move to another town and avoid being caught. What's more, criminals often changed their names and couldn't be traced. In the 1840s, photographs were added to criminal files. Yet there was no way to organize and share them in a useful or efficient way.

In 1879, a French policeman named Alphonse Bertillon developed a system known as anthropometry, the science of measuring humans. Bertillon based his system on the notion that every adult's body measurements are unique. He developed a method of taking eleven measurements of suspects. These included a person's height, the height and length of his head, the measurements of his ears, the lengths of his arms and fingers, the length of his outstretched arms, and more. Bertillon calculated that the odds of two people sharing all eleven measurements were one in 4,191,304.[1]

Bertillon's system was adopted by police precincts around the world for years. However, the training was difficult, the process was time consuming, and measurements often varied by the officer taking them. If a person's body measurements were off by a fraction of a centimeter, a case could be tossed out and a criminal could go free. By the early 1900s, the ease and speed of fingerprinting crime suspects made Bertillon's system obsolete.

ABSTRACT OF

THE ANTHROPOMETRICAL SIGNALMENT

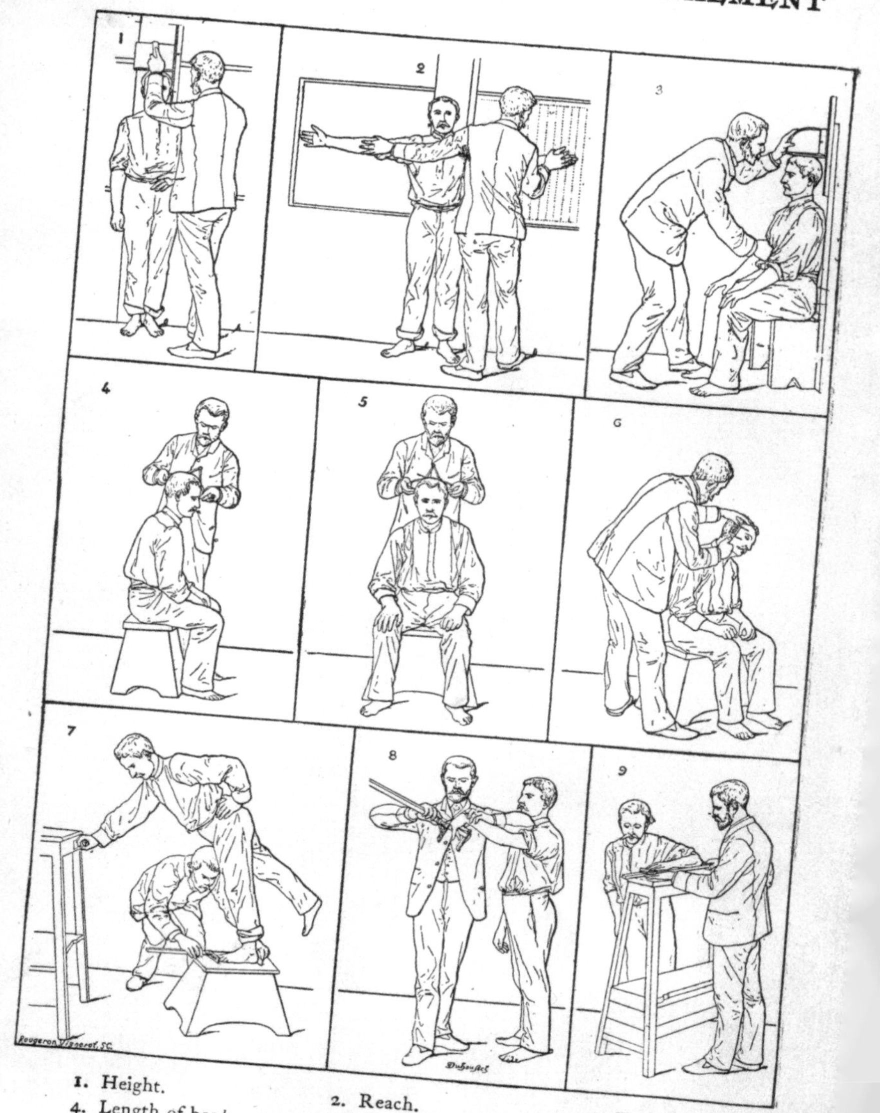

1. Height.
2. Reach.
3. Trunk.
4. Length of head.
5. Width of head.
6. Right ear.
7. Left foot.
8. Left middle finger.
9. Left forearm.

(ii)

This chart shows how police took body measurements in the late 1800s.

Police used to use body measurements to identify people.

At the time, police relied on body measurements to identify people. Basically, people were identified by many measurements, including their height, their head size, and the lengths of their arms, fingers, and feet. Incredibly, the two William Wests had body measurements that were almost identical. The guards now had two prisoners with the same name and the same appearance. How could they tell them apart?

Fortunately, a new system of identification was put in place soon afterward. The two men were fingerprinted. The clerk found that the fingerprints of the two men were different. The two William Wests were most likely identical twins who had been separated at birth.[2] Somehow they had received the same name. Despite the fact that identical twins have the same genes—making them appear virtually the same—they still have different fingerprints.

The West story has taken on legendary status in the field of crime investigation. Although the details of the West account may vary, the story shows that fingerprinting is a tried and true method of identification. It has remained a convincing tool for identifying criminals for more than one hundred years.

Get a Grip

If you decide to sleuth around your own home, you'll probably notice that fingerprints are everywhere: in smudges on the bathroom mirror, in sticky traces on the refrigerator, on a smooth computer screen, and on millions of other surfaces. The fact is, every time you leave a room, you leave your fingerprints behind.

What are those pesky prints? Why do we have them? What makes them so unique?

Fingerprints take shape as a baby grows in its mother's womb—by the nineteenth week of development. The variety of patterns of fingerprints is determined both by genes and by the movements of the baby's fingers inside the mother. Tiny movements affect the growth of dividing skin cells on each finger, causing subtle changes in fingerprints.[3] This explains why the fingerprints of identical twins, although similar, have distinct differences.

When you drag an index card or credit card across the pads of your fingers, you can feel the bumpiness of the ridges. How did these curious,

Apes also have fingerprints.

uneven surfaces evolve? Why aren't your fingertips as smooth as, say, the tip of your nose? The long-held theory is that the ridges of fingerprints evolved as a means to increase friction, the force that resists motion between two objects. Friction allows your fingertips to grip objects more firmly. Just as rubber treads enable your bicycle to grip the road or the soles of your sneakers enable your feet to cling to the pavement, fingerprint ridges help you grasp or hang on to objects.

Many of our evolutionary cousins, like tree-gripping apes, also have fingerprints. Some South American monkeys even sport ridged pads on their tails, allowing them to hang from tree branches. Picture the survival tactics that developed among ancient humans. They had to grasp spears for hunting or pick up stones to throw at dangerous predators. Without fingerprints, the theory is, our fingers might be as slippery as banana peels! People today might not be chasing away saber-toothed tigers, but without fingerprints we would have a tough time holding a fork, gripping a baseball bat, or even tying our shoes.

However, a study published in 2009 questions that theory. Roland Ennos, a biomechanicist (a scientist who studies biology and movement) at the University of Manchester in England, conducted a study on fingerprint ridges with a student, Peter Warman. Ennos hooked Warman up to a machine that measured the frictional force of a piece of acrylic glass squashing against his fingers at various angles.

The researchers discovered that fingerprints may not increase friction when we touch flat, smooth objects such as glass. The bumpy ridges and gaps between them actually cut down the amount of surface area of skin touching the glass by about 30 percent compared with smooth skin.[4] This means that fingerprint ridges reduce the skin's contact with an object. That might actually *loosen* our grip.

So if fingerprints don't increase friction, what are they for? Ennos and Warman concede that fingerprints may have evolved to increase friction with rough objects, like tree bark. Yet they also theorize that the ridges may allow our skin to be more elastic, or stretchable, like rubber. This may help protect fingertips from damage. In addition, the valleys between the ridges may allow water to drain away, like tiny canals at your fingertips. This would improve surface contact when you pick up something slippery or wet.

Another new study about the purpose of fingerprints may help researchers design better robots and artificial hands for amputees, people who have lost limbs. In 2009, researchers in France published a study in

The prints on your right hand are not the same as those on your left! In 1911, Leonardo da Vinci's famous painting, the *Mona Lisa*, was stolen. Detectives uncovered a left fingerprint of the thief. The suspect almost got away because, at the time, police mostly relied on body measurements for ID and they only kept right-hand fingerprints on file.

which they examined the function of fingerprint ridges. They hooked up a mechanical hand to sensors that responded to touch. They found that fingerprint ridges increase sensitivity at your fingertips.[5] Nerve endings in fingerprint ridges detect vibrations that result when fingertips touch something. The nerve endings connect to nerve cells that send signals to your brain. These signals may help people tell the difference between different textures (like smooth silk or rough sandpaper) or may even help us sense something potentially harmful. So when we touch something hot—*ouch!*— our fingertips sense it right away. Researchers are now exploring ways to use this research to improve sensitivity in mechanical hands. In the future, an amputee may be able to feel what a natural hand touches. A robot might be equipped to detect signs of danger in a hazardous environment, such as the surface of another planet or the inside of a nuclear reactor.

Unique by Design

Clearly, fingerprints have important functions in daily life. Yet, unless you are obsessed with cleaning the smudges off windows and mirrors, you rarely think about them. Instead, fingerprints are more notable for how they are used in modern times: for identifying people. To see what makes fingerprints unique, look closely at your prints under a strong light or magnifying lens. Notice the raised ridges? Each ridge has microscopic pores, tiny openings attached to sweat glands under the skin. Sweat is mostly water. It also contains tiny amounts of salt, amino acids (proteins), and other chemicals. When your fingers sweat or you touch a substance like oil, food, dirt, blood, or grease and then press your fingers against a surface, you transfer the substance to that surface. That leaves an outline of the ridge patterns behind. These are your fingerprints—your unique signature. When you steal a cookie from the cookie jar and

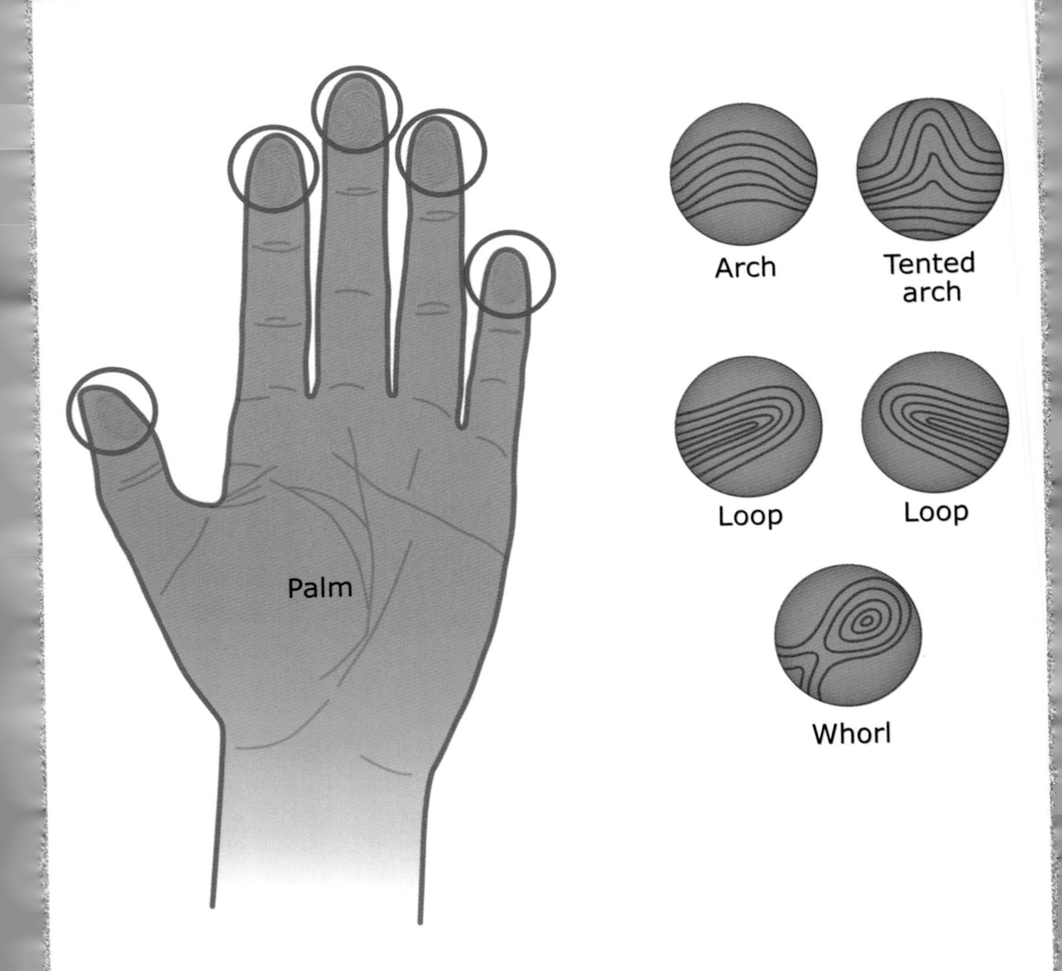

You will find patterns of lines at the end of each finger. The basic fingerprint patterns are arch, loop, and whorl.

Fingertip ridges have tiny pores, as seen in this magnified photograph. Each pore leads to a sweat gland under the skin.

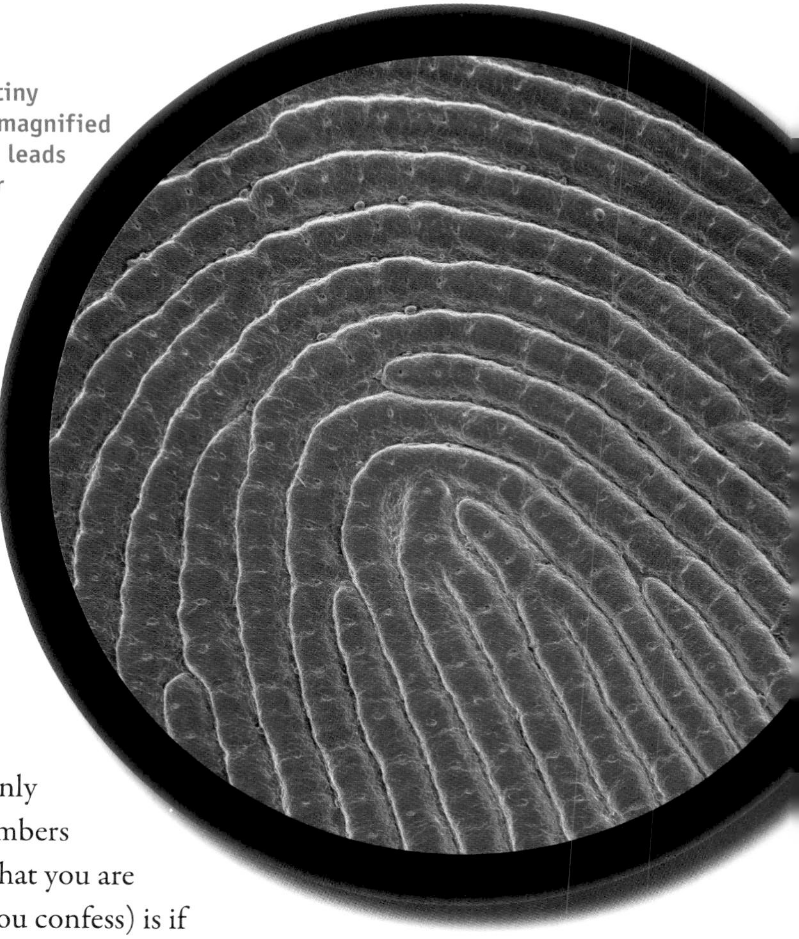

leave a fingerprint behind, it's almost like leaving a note that says, "I ate the last cookie."

Of course, the only way your family members would *really* know that you are the culprit (unless you confess) is if they matched your unique fingerprint to the one left on the cookie jar. What makes every person's prints so different from each other? Ridge patterns. Fingerprint ridges and the valleys between them—called furrows—twist around to form countless unique designs.

When experts classify fingerprints, they look at three basic ridge patterns: loops, whorls, and arches. Loops are the most common patterns. Experts encounter loops in about two-thirds of the fingerprints they analyze. Whorls appear in about one-third of fingerprints. Arches, the least common pattern, occur only in about 5 percent of fingerprints.[6]

Each of these categories also has subcategories. An arch, for example, can be plain (rounded like a hill) or tented (pointed at the top like a traffic cone).

MORE MINUTIAE

FOLLOWING IS SOME "loopy lingo" you might hear crime scene investigators use to describe fingerprints:

bifurcation: The place where a ridge divides into two (also called a fork).

bridge: A connecting ridge between two parallel-running ridges.

core: The approximate center of a fingerprint's ridge pattern.

delta: A triangular ridge pattern.

divergence: The place where ridges split apart after running parallel.

dot: A ridge that doesn't display direction; its length approximates its width.

enclosure: A ridge that splits and then rejoins.

end: The point where a ridge starts or stops.

focal point: An identical point of comparison between two fingerprints.

island: A small ridge section located between other, longer ridges.

ridge count: The number of ridges that run between the core and delta focal points.

The ridges of a loop start at one side of the fingertip, loop around, and then return to the same side. Loops can either be ulnar (pointing toward the pinky finger) or radial (pointing toward the thumb).

Whorls have spiral or circular patterns, like the giant lollipops you see at a fair. Sometimes whorls have pockets, a tight swirl of ridges at the center. They may also form a double loop, a pattern in which two whorls collide in the center.

When studying prints, examiners look for focal points, or identical points of comparison between two prints. Experts may begin by locating two focal points: a core (the center of a pattern) and a delta (a triangular pattern where ridges divide). They then record the number of ridges between the core and delta, or between two deltas. A loop has one core and one delta. A whorl has two or more deltas. An arch has no core or delta.

Cores and deltas are examples of minutiae (min OOH shuh), the tiny variations in a fingerprint. Minutiae make each fingerprint truly unique. Fingerprints can vary by the number, types, and positions of ridges and minutiae. In the United States, forensic labs differ on the number of corresponding points that are required to make a match between two prints. Some labs have made a match with as few as eight points. Most rely on about ten matching points. In England, experts must find sixteen corresponding points in order to make a match.[7]

With all of the possible variations in fingerprints, you can see why no two fingerprints have been found to be exactly the same. So, if someone suspects that you're the cookie crook and can back up his accusation with fingerprint evidence, you might want to wipe the crumbs off your mouth and turn yourself in.

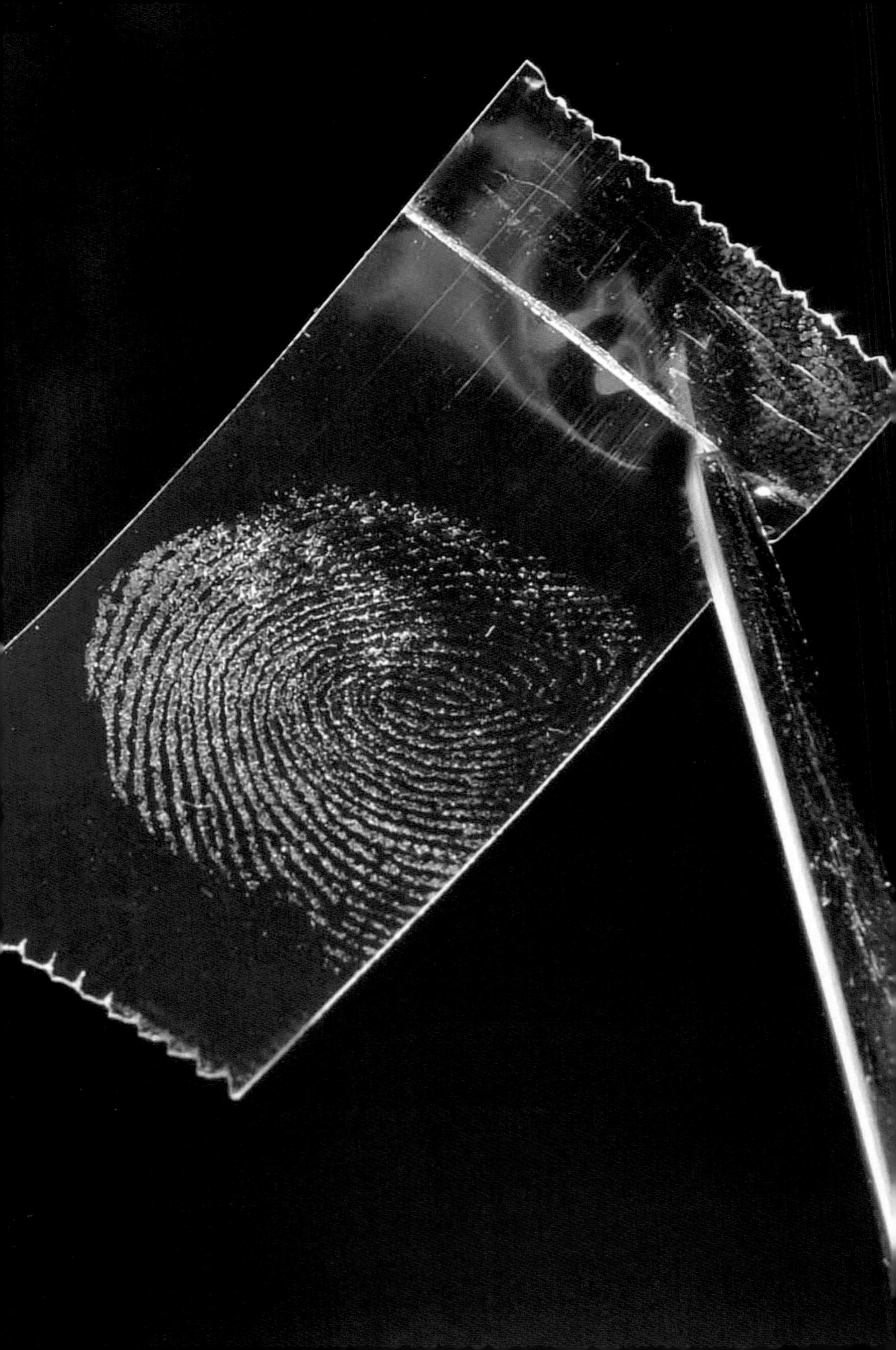

How fingerprints became instant ID

On September 18, 1910, before daybreak, Clarence Hiller awoke to find a stranger in his Chicago home. The two men struggled and tumbled down a flight of stairs. The intruder fired two shots, killing Hiller, and then fled.

Soon afterward, police arrested a suspect, Thomas Jennings, less than a mile from Hiller's home. He was found carrying a loaded gun and was covered with bloodstains. Jennings claimed the blood had come from injuries he had gotten when falling from a streetcar.

Police collected evidence at Hiller's home, including unused bullets and traces of gravel and sand. However, the key evidence that sent Jennings to jail was a set of fingerprints found in the kitchen. On the day before he was murdered,

Hiller had painted some stair rails next to a window. When Jennings broke into Hiller's home through that window, he had touched the wet paint and left a set of four fingerprints.

The Chicago police department compared Jennings's prints to those found at the crime scene. They were a match. In 1911, Jennings was found guilty of murder and was executed. The Jennings case marks the first murder conviction in the United States based on fingerprint evidence.

Fingerprint History

Today it seems so routine: Detectives check a crime scene for fingerprints, and suspects are fingerprinted after being arrested. Like mug shots (photos of suspects), fingerprints have become a standard of identification. But it wasn't always that way. Fingerprinting has been evolving as a source of criminal identification for more than a century. In fact, the steps leading up to Thomas Jennings's conviction based on fingerprint evidence (and the millions of cases since then) stretch way back in history—for hundreds, even thousands, of years.

Archaeologists claim that long before humans could write, potters "signed" their work by making impressions of their fingerprints in clay. Around 2000 B.C., Babylonians used fingerprints to sign contracts. Ancient Chinese legal documents and criminal confessions from around the year 1000 B.C. were also endorsed with fingerprints.

Alfred Stratton and his brother Albert were the first men in Britain to be convicted on the basis of fingerprint evidence. Albert was connected to a murder due to a fingerprint left on a cash box at the crime scene(top right) which matched his own (bottom right). The brothers were found guilty of murder.

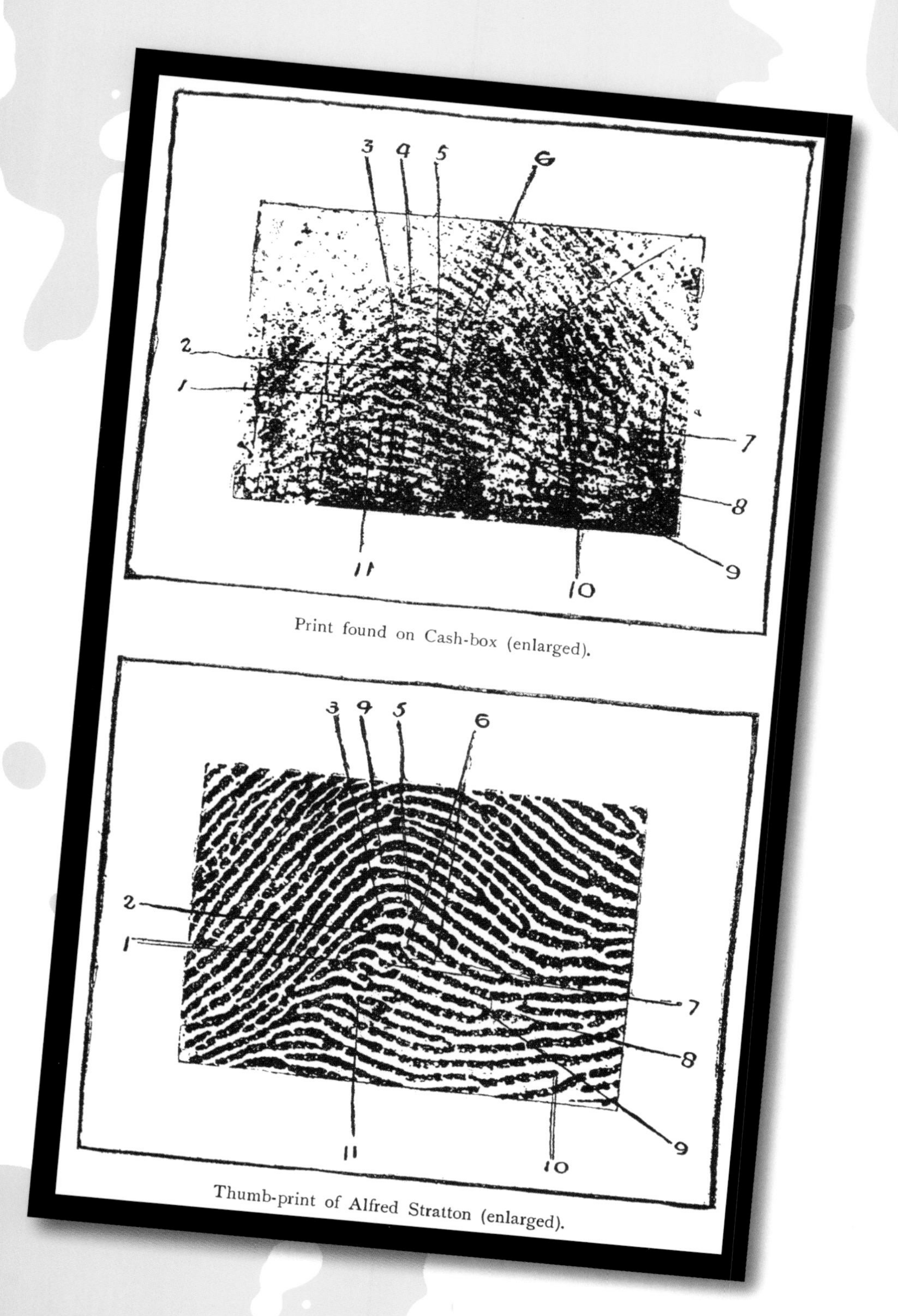

Print found on Cash-box (enlarged).

Thumb-print of Alfred Stratton (enlarged).

Clearly, early civilizations knew that fingerprints were distinctive. Yet it took several centuries for people to begin classifying the unique patterns of fingerprints. In 1686, an Italian biologist named Marcello Malpighi became the first person to describe the ridges in fingerprints as loops and whorls. In 1823, a Czech physiologist named Johan Evangelista Purkinje published a book about skin. It included descriptions of nine different fingerprint types and methods for identifying them.

In India in 1858, Sir William James Herschel, a British government official, had workers "sign" contracts by inking and stamping their palms and fingerprints. Herschel used this technique because not all employees could sign their own names. In addition, those who could sign would sometimes deny that the signatures were their own. Over time, Herschel noticed that no two prints were the same. He also realized that a person's prints never changed with age. Herschel's print files became the first modern example in which fingerprints were used for the purpose of identification. Yet there was still a leap from signing contracts to solving crimes.

In the late 1870s, Henry Faulds, a Scottish physician and missionary working in Tokyo, Japan, became fascinated by fingerprints. Around 1878, he became interested in fingerprints left on ancient pottery that had been discovered at an archaeological dig near his hospital. Like Herschel, Faulds began collecting fingerprints of the people around him. He and his medical students also tried to rub off their fingerprints with knives, sandpaper, and other substances. They discovered that the prints grew back in exactly the same pattern as before.

Soon afterward, Faulds heard about a robbery. He used his newfound knowledge of fingerprints to help solve the crime. He even used fingerprints to prove a man's innocence. He showed police that a suspect's prints did not match a print found on the wall next to a building that had been robbed. In 1880, Faulds sent his observations to *Nature,* a prestigious British journal. "When bloody finger marks or impressions on clay, glass, etc. exist, they may lead to the scientific identification of criminals."[1]

LITERATURE LINK

In *Life on the Mississippi* (1883), author Mark Twain describes how a murderer was identified by fingerprint evidence. In 1894, Twain wrote the book *Pudd'nHead Wilson*, in which a trial hinges on fingerprint evidence. These books were published twenty years before fingerprinting criminals became routine in the United States.

Faulds was right on the mark. Although it took many years for Faulds to get credit for his work, it was only a matter of time before fingerprinting criminals caught on. As you read in Chapter 1, police in the late 1800s relied on a system of body measurements for identifying criminals. Then, in 1892, a British scientist named Francis Galton became convinced that fingerprinting would be the wave of the future.

Galton came from a wealthy and well-known family of scientists. One of his cousins was Charles Darwin, who developed the theory of evolution by natural selection. Galton published a book called *Finger Prints* in which he described a detailed system of classifying fingerprints based on arches, loops, and whorls. He claimed that his fingerprint system could help identify military recruits, missing persons, and travelers. He also showed how investigators could save fingerprints found at a crime scene and later match them to prints from another case. Galton calculated that the odds of finding two people with identical fingerprints was one in 64 billion.

In 1900, Edward Henry, inspector-general of police in Bengal, India, published a book that made classifying fingerprints more user-friendly. The book, *The Classification and Uses of Finger Prints*, became very popular in police bureaus around the world. Henry's basic system served

THE HENRY SYSTEM OF CLASSIFICATION

VERSIONS OF THE HENRY SYSTEM of Classification have been used to sort fingerprints for nearly one hundred years, from 1900 until the 1990s. The system groups prints based on loops, whorls, and arches. Each finger is assigned a number, beginning with the right thumb as number 1 and ending with the left pinky as number 10. Numbers are then assigned to fingers that have a whorl pattern. For example, if fingers 1 or 2 have a whorl pattern, they each receive a value of 16. Fingers 3 and 4 each have a value of 8. Fingers 5 and 6 each have a value of 4. Fingers 7 and 8 each have a value of 2 and Fingers 9 and 10 have a value of zero. Loop and arch patterns also receive a value of zero.

The examiner then adds the number values of whorls on even-numbered fingers and adds one. Then he or she adds the values for odd-numbered fingers, plus one. The examiner records the two sums as a fraction, for example 15/2. This individual's prints are then filed in a group of other prints that also received 15/2. The fraction 1/1 indicates that no fingers have whorl patterns. The fraction 32/32 shows that all fingers have whorl patterns. Categorizing fingerprints with a system like this cuts down on the need to scour through every fingerprint on file.

However, the Henry System only works when all ten fingerprints are available, something rarely found at a crime scene. Today, the automated, computerized fingerprint system run by the FBI no longer relies on the Henry System. The new system classifies fingerprints according to the distance measured from a core to a delta, the locations of minutiae, types of patterns present, and other descriptive information.

as the basis for modern-day fingerprint classification until the 1990s. Because of his work, Henry was appointed assistant commissioner of Scotland Yard (the London police) and head of the Criminal Investigation Department (CID). The CID opened a fingerprint bureau in 1901. The next year, relying on fingerprint evidence, the bureau arrested 1,722 repeat offenders. One can only imagine the excitement that must have spread when they discovered that that number was nearly four times the number of repeat criminals that the body-measurement system had identified in its most successful year. A new criminal identification system was born.

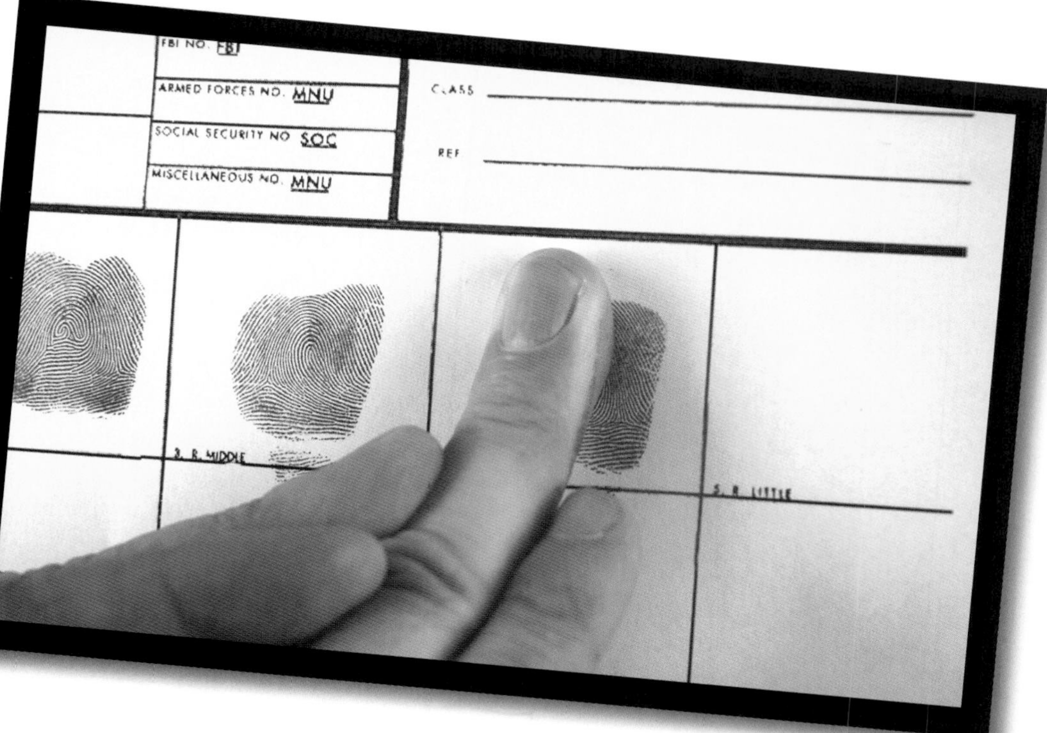

All ten fingerprints are recorded on a fingerprint card. The Henry System of Classification was based on having a record of all ten prints, which does not usually happen at a crime scene.

Fast Forward

In 1903, the New York City police department became the first in the United States to fingerprint suspects. At the World's Fair in St. Louis in 1904, fingerprint experts from Scotland Yard trained American police officers to collect and analyze fingerprints. By 1910, the year that Thomas Jennings killed Clarence Hiller, fingerprinting had become routine in police precincts across the country. Before his execution, however, Jennings's lawyers tried to appeal his conviction. They challenged the Supreme Court of Illinois on the grounds that fingerprint evidence should not be accepted as evidence. In a landmark ruling, the Illinois Supreme Court stated, "There is a scientific basis for the system of

Before the 1960s, the FBI kept fingerprints on individual cards. Each card had to be reviewed manually. Computers changed all this!

fingerprint identification, and . . . the courts are justified in admitting this class of evidence."[2] Jennings's fate was sealed. His case made fingerprinting in criminal cases a more accepted practice around the world.

In 1924, Congress established the FBI's Identification Division to collect and catalogue fingerprint files from across the nation. For the first time, using the unique patterns in fingerprints, police could link a robber who had committed a crime in one place to a theft he had carried out in another place at a different time.

In the beginning, comparing fingerprints on notecards was a painstaking job. Sorting through thousands of fingerprints by hand could take months. Suspects were often released before a match could be made. Fortunately, in the 1960s, investigators began using computers to help match fingerprints. In the 1970s, the FBI established the Automated

Computerized fingerprint databases now make catalogued fingerprints much easier to search.

This portable fingerprint scanner can be used to do instant fingerprint checks at the scene of a crime.

FINGERPRINTING: THEN AND NOW

DACTYLOSCOPY IS A FANCY WORD for the technique of obtaining someone's fingerprints. To take a person's fingerprints the traditional, old-fashioned way, all you need is ink and a card. First, the suspect's fingertips are cleaned with alcohol to remove sweat and dirt. Then his fingers are coated in black ink to cover the entire ridge area. Each fingertip is rolled onto a card from one side of the fingernail to the other. These prints are called rolled fingerprints. Next, the suspect presses down all ten fingers (each hand at a forty-five-degree angle) to make flat prints. In the days before computers, fingerprint cards were organized in filing cabinets based on their ridge patterns. They were mailed from precinct to precinct to identify criminals. Today these prints are scanned, saved, and shared on a nationwide computer database.

The modern, high-tech way to take fingerprints uses Live Scan, a digital scanner. No messy ink is necessary. A person lays his or her fingers flat on a scanner. In a matter of seconds the scanner converts the scanned prints into a digital picture. A computer marks notable features of the fingerprints (e.g., whorls, arches, loops, and minutiae) that can be used to identify them. Fingerprint scans are stored on the FBI's nationwide database and can be shared instantly. Many police precincts have been outfitted with Live Scan technology. As costs for these machines go down, digital fingerprinting will become standard across the country. Two thumbs up!

Sarah Geronimo, a celebrity from the Philippines, gets her fingerprint scanned in order to obtain a visa to visit the United States.

Fingerprint Identification System (AFIS), a computerized system that collects criminal histories and provides automated fingerprint matches. In 1992, the Identification Division became the Criminal Justice Information Services Division.

In 1999, the FBI cranked it up a notch. They began using the Integrated Automated Fingerprint Identification System (IAFIS), which joined together AFIS databases from around the country. IAFIS stores and exchanges fingerprint data 24/7, with criminal histories of more than 55 million people.[3] Several thousand new records are added each day. The FBI has the largest collection of fingerprints in the world, with more than 200 million fingerprints on file.[4] For each search, computers run through millions of possibilities and display the prints most likely to match. IAFIS has cut down on the time it takes to make a fingerprint match from months or weeks to hours and minutes. Forensic experts must then closely examine the prints to make the final call.

As of now, FBI computers receive requests for fingerprint data from crime labs across the United States and Canada every second. Fingerprints are processed and matches are made (or not) at a mind-boggling pace—as often as a hundred thousand times per day.[5] Technology is now available for police to perform computerized fingerprint checks at the scene of a crime. Theoretically, a police officer could pull over a speeding car, scan the driver's prints, and run an instant, computerized fingerprint check. Within moments, the officer would know if the person was a wanted criminal or on a database of the FBI's most-wanted criminals or terrorists.

ID FOR THE DEAD

SOMETIMES investigators need to fingerprint a dead body to identify it. The problem: When skin dries out, it shrivels. That makes fingerprinting nearly impossible. To soften up the skin, investigators may soak the fingertips in water or heat them with a microwave. Sometimes they inject the fingertips with chemical "tissue builder" to plump them up. If a body was in water for a long time, the skin can be badly damaged. In this case, an investigator may peel the skin off the dead person's fingers and then wear the skin like a glove to make a print.

In addition, smudged fingerprints that are collected at the scene of a crime can be digitally enhanced and "cleaned up." Computers help change lighting and contrast to make prints that were once hard to read jump off the screen. All of this information helps police catch criminals faster than ever. The bottom line: The twenty-first century isn't a good time to try to get away with crime.

How do experts locate and lift prints?

On February 9, 1996, a huge truck bomb ripped through Canary Wharf, a business and shopping district in London, England. The blast killed two people and injured thirty-nine others. The bomb caused $225 million in damage. The bombing ended a seventeen-month ceasefire between Britain and the Irish Republican Army (IRA). British security forces were caught off guard.

Scotland Yard's antiterrorist unit fanned out to search for suspects. Little evidence remained; the site of the

A truck bomb caused millions of dollars of damage to Canary Wharf, a business and shopping district in London, on February 9, 1996.

This police officer is dusting with powder to find hidden fingerprints.

bombing was a massive crater in the ground. The main lead came from a police officer who had seen the truck—a Ford flatbed—before it exploded. When newspapers published a picture of the truck, one witness called to say he had seen the vehicle parked ten miles from the bomb site just days before the blast. Two men had been seen unloading a trailer that the truck had been hauling.

Investigators found the trailer parked in an empty lot. Next to it was a tire filled with garbage. To a good detective, searching though garbage can be like digging for gold. In this case, investigators found a chart that tracked the truck's travels from England to Northern Ireland and back. Police also traced the trail back to a motel in Carlisle, England, where the bombers had apparently stayed twice.

Investigators combed the motel for evidence. Although the rooms had been cleaned since the bombing, detectives checked for fingerprints. As in any crime scene, the investigators knew that prints could be left on virtually any surface. Some prints, called patent prints, are visible to the naked eye. These are the smudgy fingerprints left by dirty or sweaty fingers. Patent prints can usually be photographed or lifted with special tape. Others fingerprints are called plastic prints. They are 3-D, molded impressions of prints left in clay, soap, wet paint, wax, wet cement, or other soft or sticky materials. Many prints, however, are not visible. These are called latent prints. These prints may be found on glass, plastic bags, paper, or any number of surfaces.

How can you "see" invisible prints? Crime scene investigators are trained to apply more than forty techniques to uncover and retrieve fingerprints without destroying them. They use a variety of powders, chemicals, gases, or special lights and lasers to expose them. The most common technique involves dusting a surface with fine, black powder. When the powder sticks to the oily, greasy impressions left by a person's touch, a fingerprint appears. Technicians use different kinds of powders to make fingerprints pop out on different colored surfaces. They then photograph them and "lift" the prints for comparison using special tools or sticky tape.

At the motel in Carlisle, England, detectives uncovered one hundred prints. Then they fingerprinted the motel's staff to rule them out as suspects. One latent thumb print, found on an ashtray, gave investigators a lead. It didn't match any of the motel staff.

To uncover the print, the investigators used a technique called superglue fuming. Superglue is strong, fast-acting glue made from an adhesive called cyanoacrylate. Chemicals in the glue stick to amino acids (proteins) left on a surface by a fingerprint. Technicians place the object under investigation in an airtight tank along with a small heater. They put a few drops of superglue in a dish, seal the tank, and crank up the heat. As the superglue heats up, it turns into a gas. Its particles stick to the amino acids in a fingerprint. The result? A visible fingerprint coated in white residue appears. The dried glue makes it hard to smudge. Investigators dust on some powder to make the print stand out even more.

The superglue-enhanced thumbprint found on the ashtray at the motel in Carlisle gave investigators their first clue. Meanwhile, other investigators had been carefully sorting through the garbage found near the trailer. They discovered a meal voucher from a ferry that had carried the truck from Northern Ireland to England. No fingerprints were visible on the voucher, but it was possible that a suspect had touched it.

The problem is that porous (or absorbent) surfaces such as paper or cardboard absorb the sweat in fingerprints, leaving the marks invisible. The challenge is to make a latent print appear without destroying the paper. To accomplish this, investigators usually use chemical substances that react with other chemicals found in sweat. Two of these substances are called ninhydrin and DFO (or, as a

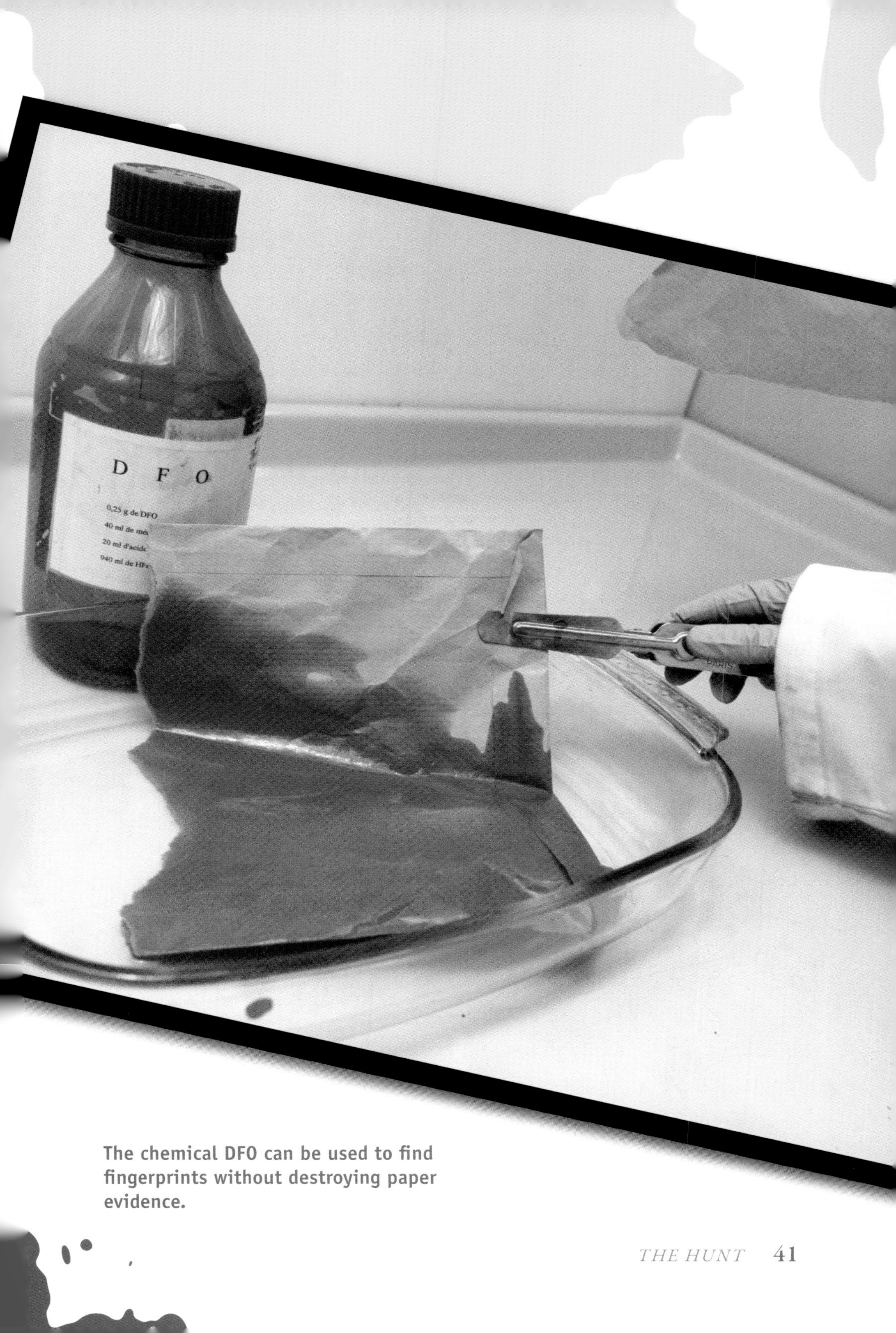

The chemical DFO can be used to find fingerprints without destroying paper evidence.

chemist might call it, 1,8-Diazafluoren-9-one). Investigators either spray a piece of evidence with one of these chemical solutions, or dip it in one. Then they warm the evidence in an oven. Fingerprints treated with ninhydrin appear purple. Those treated with DFO glow when lit by a laser or blue-green light. After treating the meal voucher with both ninhydrin and DFO, police uncovered a second clue—another faint thumbprint. It matched the print on the ashtray from the motel.

Surprisingly, a third matching thumbprint was found on a copy of *Truck & Driver* magazine. It had been left out in the rain near the trailer for two weeks. To uncover that print, lab techs used physical developer, a solution of silver and iron compounds. These compounds are known to reveal prints on porous surfaces that have been soaked in water.

Now Scotland Yard had three thumbprints from the same person, linking him to the bombing. They nicknamed their suspect "Triple Thumbprint Man." Hot on the trail, investigators ran the thumbprints through their computer database. No match was found. The IRA had chosen an operative with no criminal record. His thumbprints could not be traced. The investigation screeched to a halt.

Several months later, the British Army's Special Forces arrested a group of IRA terrorists suspected of carrying out sniper shootings. One of the shooters was James McArdle, a bricklayer and truck driver from Ireland. Investigators ran McArdle's fingerprints through their computer system and compared them with the London bomber. They matched! James McArdle was the notorious Triple Thumbprint Man.

McArdle's trial in June 1998 laid out the details of the fatal bombing. Lawyers showed how the bomber made trips from Ireland to England as a practice for the attack. Terrorists had packed the truck with more than a ton of explosives. The fingerprint evidence was enough to tie McArdle to the crime. On June 25, 1998, Triple Thumbprint Man received a sentence of twenty-five years in prison for "conspiracy to cause

explosions." However, McArdle served only two years in prison. In 2000, he was released as part of a new peace agreement between the IRA and the British government.

Fingerprinting Mess-up Nabs JFK's Assassin

As you've seen, crime scene investigators are trained to use a wide variety of techniques to uncover fingerprints. Their job is tricky because if they use the wrong technique they could end up destroying evidence. However, in at least one notorious case, a mistake in exposing prints led to the identification of an infamous killer.

November 22, 1963, was one of the darkest days in American history. On that day, during a parade in Dallas, Texas, President John F. Kennedy was assassinated. Police raced to find the killer. Less than two hours after the shooting, police found a rifle lying next to a window in the Texas Book Depository, a building that overlooked the parade route. Cardboard boxes were stacked around the window. The police checked for fingerprints. A right palm print was found on the rifle. Fingerprints also were found on the cardboard boxes and on a paper bag.

The prints matched a man named Lee Harvey Oswald. A complicating factor was that Oswald worked in the Book Depository building. Oswald could have left the prints on the boxes and bag at any time. In addition, someone could have placed the rifle by the window to frame him. The police needed to prove that these were fresh prints left at the scene at the time when Kennedy was killed. Unlike some other kinds of evidence (such as a dead body), fingerprints can't be dated. That is, fingerprints can't tell you when a crime may have occurred. Yet in this case, something unexpected happened. Dallas detectives had made a mistake when they were checking for prints. Their mix-up, however, would lead to success.

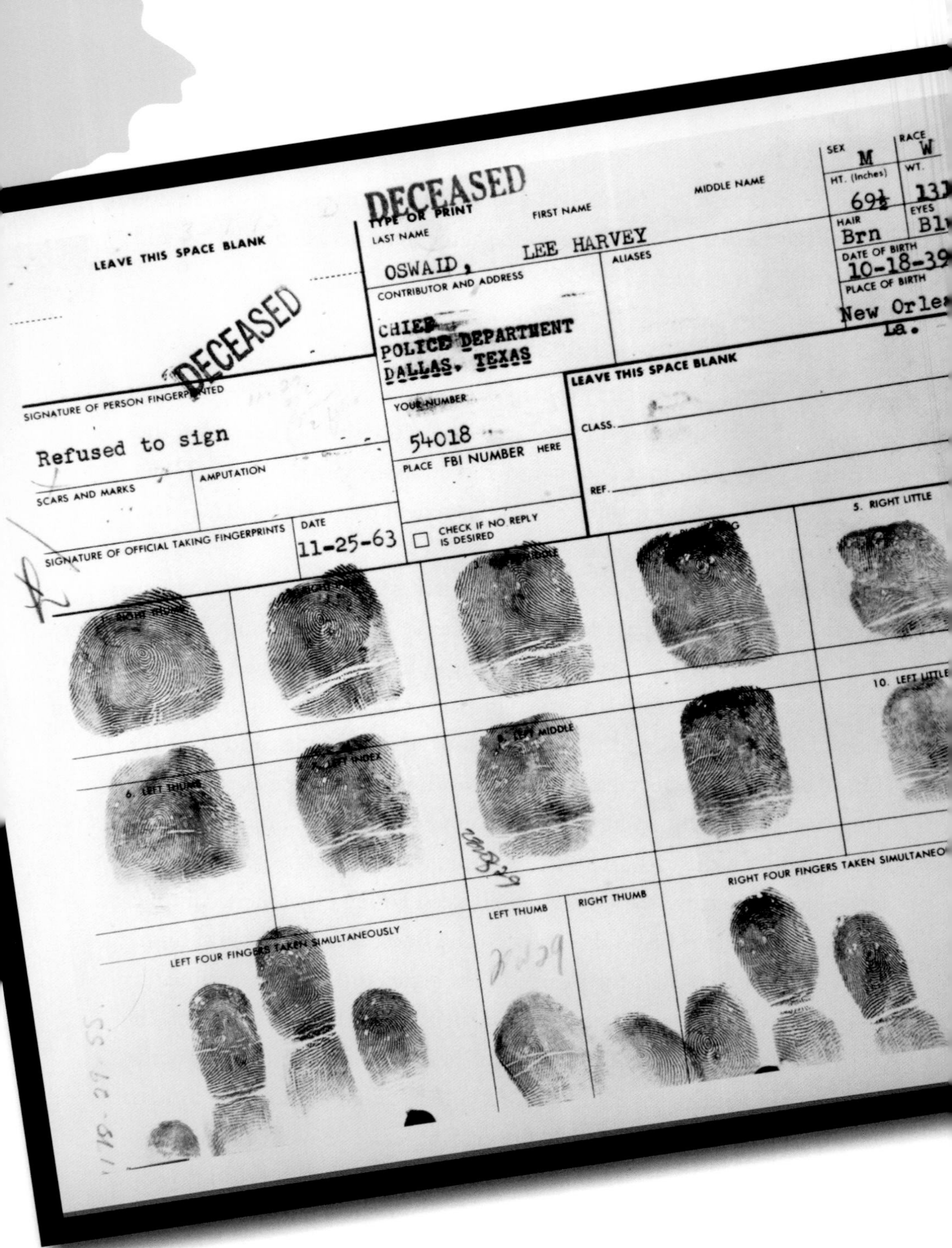
DECEASED

LEAVE THIS SPACE BLANK

DECEASED

TYPE OR PRINT

LAST NAME: OSWALD,

FIRST NAME: LEE

MIDDLE NAME: HARVEY

SEX: M

RACE: W

HT. (Inches): 69½

WT.: 13[illegible]

HAIR: Brn

EYES: Bl[illegible]

DATE OF BIRTH: 10-18-39

PLACE OF BIRTH: New Orle[illegible] La.

CONTRIBUTOR AND ADDRESS: CHIEF POLICE DEPARTMENT DALLAS, TEXAS

ALIASES

SIGNATURE OF PERSON FINGERPRINTED: Refused to sign

YOUR NUMBER: 54018

PLACE FBI NUMBER HERE

LEAVE THIS SPACE BLANK

CLASS.

REF.

SCARS AND MARKS

AMPUTATION

SIGNATURE OF OFFICIAL TAKING FINGERPRINTS

DATE: 11-25-63

☐ CHECK IF NO REPLY IS DESIRED

1. RIGHT THUMB

2. RIGHT INDEX

3. RIGHT MIDDLE

4. RIGHT RING

5. RIGHT LITTLE

6. LEFT THUMB

7. LEFT INDEX

8. LEFT MIDDLE

10. LEFT LITTLE

LEFT FOUR FINGERS TAKEN SIMULTANEOUSLY

LEFT THUMB

RIGHT THUMB

RIGHT FOUR FINGERS TAKEN SIMULTANEO[illegible]

Lee Harvey Oswald's fingerprint card, dated November 25, 1963.

VANISHING PRINTS

THE FINGERPRINTS OF children often disappear before they can be detected by police. For some reason, the fatty acids in children's prints evaporate more quickly than those in the prints of adults.

Cardboard is a porous, or absorbent, surface—like paper. As you read in the London bomber case, the correct way to check for latent prints on cardboard is to treat it with chemicals such as ninhydrin. Yet the Dallas detectives used dusting powder by accident. Dusting powder is usually used only on solid, nonporous surfaces like glass. Still, the detectives managed to uncover several prints. How did that happen?

Crime lab investigators in Washington, D.C., examined the boxes more closely. They brushed dusting powder on similar boxes. To their surprise, dusting powder uncovered fingerprints for up to three hours after prints had been left. After that, the cardboard absorbed the moisture in the prints, causing them to disappear. A lightbulb went off for the investigators: Oswald's prints were uncovered by police dusting the cardboard in the first three hours after the assassination. So Oswald had to have been standing at the window at the time Kennedy was killed. With other evidence mounting against Oswald, detectives knew he was their man.

Sometimes it takes a little bit of luck to find fingerprints. Yet crime scene investigators know they can't rely on luck alone. They need good skills, lots of experience, and a great deal of knowledge to figure out which techniques will work best to locate and uncover prints. "Part of your training in processing evidence is becoming familiar with the different techniques, what they react to, and what the best methods will be," says Lyla Thompson, supervisor of the Latent Print Section at the Johnson County Crime Lab in Mission, Kansas. "As a professional, you learn to use the technique that you think will work best."[1]

FINDING FINGERPRINTS

HOW ARE CRIME SCENE INVESTIGATORS (CSIs) like magicians? They make invisible fingerprints appear! Here are some of the forty techniques they use to make it happen:

DUSTING POWDER

Surface: Nonporous (non-absorbent) surfaces, including walls, windows, doors, and furniture

How it works: CSIs use soft brushes to dust a surface with a fine powder, such as finely ground aluminum. The powder sticks to the moisture left behind by oily, sweaty, or sticky fingers. Different colored powders make prints appear on different backgrounds.

Cool fact: Some "handy" places to dust for prints: the rearview mirror of a car; the underside of a toilet seat (for men's prints); dirty dishes and silverware.

DFO (1,8-DIAZAFLUOREN-9-ONE)

Surface: Porous (absorbent) surfaces, such as paper or cardboard

How it works: DFO makes prints glow when lit by a laser or blue-green light. DFO is 100 times more sensitive than ninhydrin, but ultraviolet (UV) light is needed to make prints treated with DFO appear.

Cool fact: Adding heat improves results. If a lab oven is not available, investigators can use a toaster oven, hair dryer, or dry iron.

GENTIAN VIOLET

Surface: Sticky adhesives like tape and labels; wide variety of surfaces

How it works: Gentian violet is known to stain skin. When a solution of gentian violet is applied to a surface, it dyes dead skin cells or fatty deposits left by a fingerprint, making the print appear purple.

Cool fact: Gentian violet contains phenol, which is poisonous and can be absorbed through skin. Experts must always wear gloves and protective clothing when handling this substance.

ALTERNATE LIGHT SOURCES (OR FORENSIC LIGHTS)

Surface: Multiple surfaces, including paper, fabric, and skin

How it works: In a darkened room, investigators focus a laser on a surface. The light illuminates a fingerprint without altering the print or leaving any residue. Fluorescent powders sometimes help make prints more visible. One drawback is cost. One machine used in an FBI fingerprint lab costs $65,000.[2]

Cool fact: This technique was discovered by accident. In the 1970s, Canadian researchers noticed that when they turned on lasers, their fingerprints kept getting in the way. Their annoyance turned into a major breakthrough for fingerprint detection.

NINHYDRIN

Surface: Porous surfaces, including paper and cardboard; wallpaper

How it works: Ninhydrin reacts with traces of amino acids in a fingerprint. Heat makes the process work faster. Sometimes technicians iron surfaces treated with ninhydrin to speed up the process. When lit up, ninhydrin makes prints appear purple.

Cool fact: This technique has been in use since 1954. Ninhydrin is the most common chemical used for developing prints on paper. It has been used to develop prints that are more than fifty years old.

RUVIS (REFLECTED ULTRAVIOLET IMAGING SYSTEM)

Surface: Most smooth, nonporous surfaces, including plastic bags, the sticky side of tape, glossy magazines, photographs, credit cards, compact discs, linoleum tile, etc.

How it works: RUVIS works like a portable laser. It uses a special UV light to illuminate a print, which can then be photographed with UV-sensitive film.

Cool fact: RUVIS can be used to find prints on skin.

SUPERGLUE (CYANOACRYLATE) FUMING

Surface: Nonporous surfaces, including metal, glass, aluminum foil, rubber bands, Styrofoam, and plastic products; also some porous surfaces

How it works: In an airtight space, superglue is heated in a beaker. The glue vaporizes. As it condenses, crystals stick to the oils or sweat in fingerprints, leaving a white residue that makes an image appear. Dyes or powders are often added to make the prints stand out.

Cool fact: In 1978, the Japanese National Police Agency became the first to use superglue as an agent to make latent prints visible.

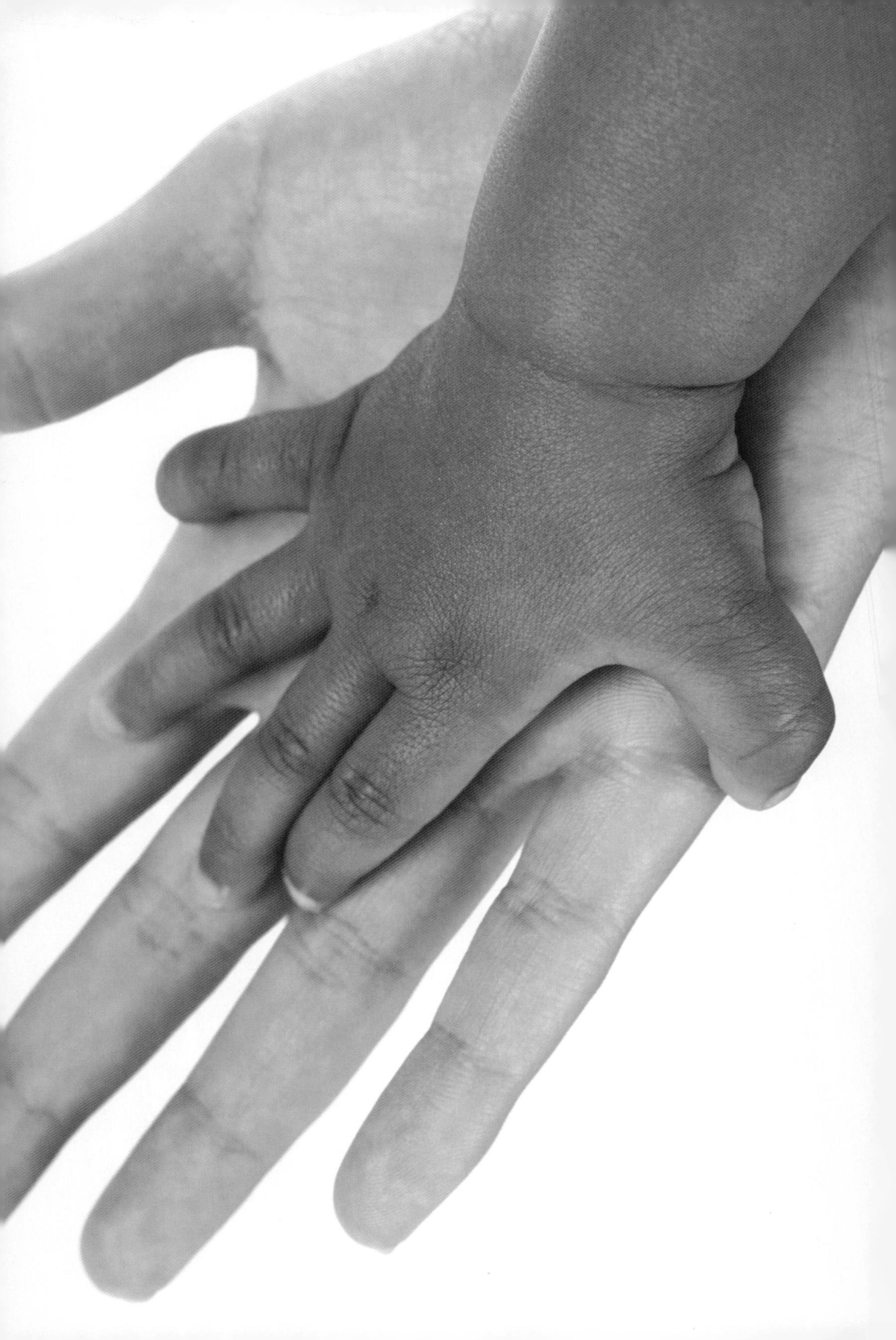

You Can Run, But You Can't Hide

How fingerprints catch up with criminals

As you grow old, many things about your body change. Your hair turns gray or thins out, your skin wrinkles, your bones may become brittle, your teeth might fall out. Yet your fingerprints never change as long as you live. They form on the pads of your fingers before you are born. As your body grows, your tiny fingers grow to adult size. Yet from babyhood through adulthood, the patterns in your fingerprints never change. Your fingerprints are yours . . . *forever*.

This fact makes fingerprints very handy tools for nabbing criminals. If someone commits a crime at a young age and leaves a fingerprint behind, the person could still be connected to the crime years later because his fingerprints never change. Many people either don't know this fact or they

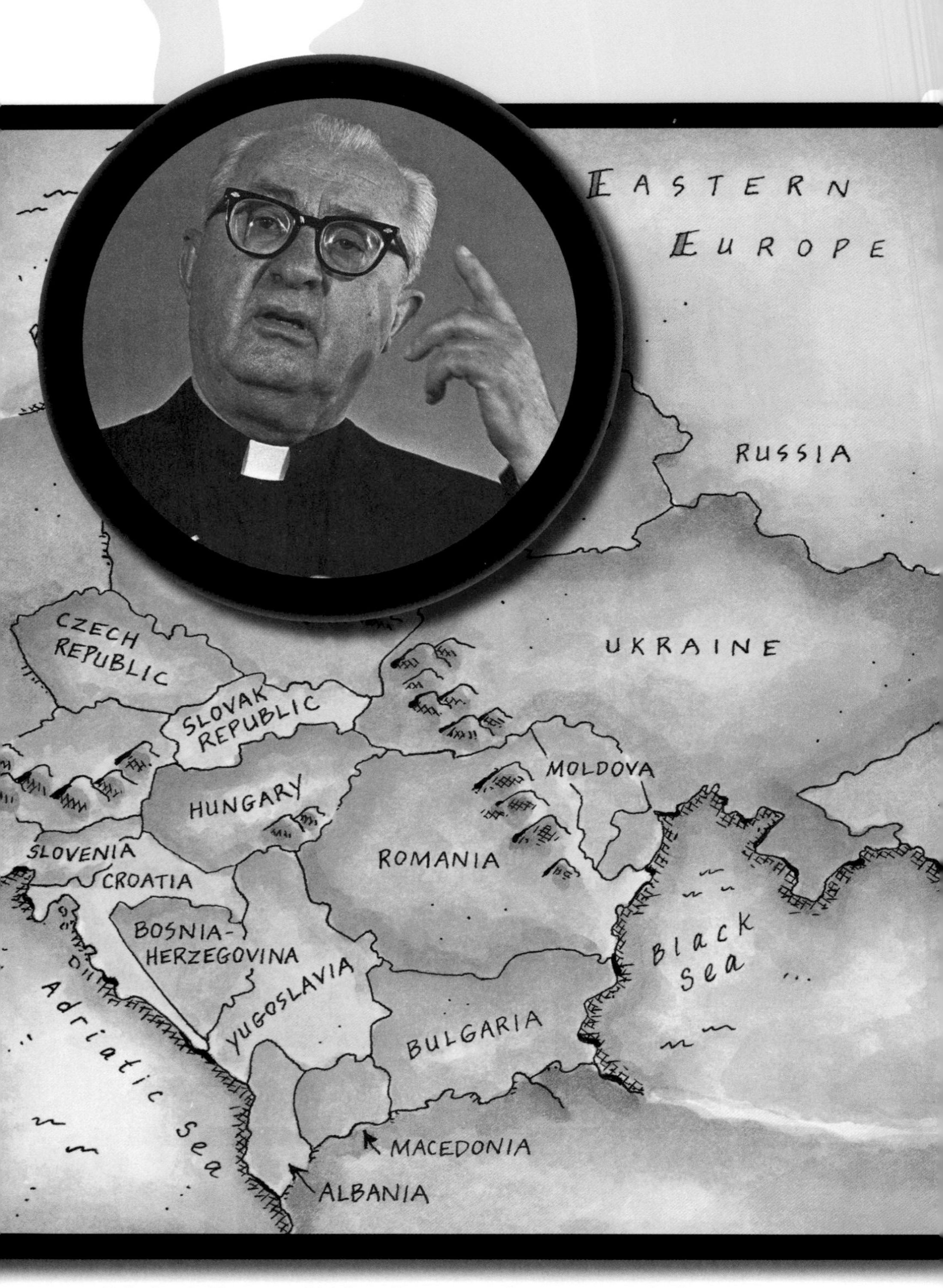

Valerian Trifa, an archbishop from Romania, was accused of war crimes based on fingerprint evidence.

forget about it when they commit a crime. They may live their whole lives thinking they can get away with murder—literally. But chances are that they left some evidence behind. The two cases described in this chapter involve individuals who committed crimes in their twenties, but paid their dues more than forty years later when law officers used fingerprint evidence against them.

Case #1: Pointing a Finger at a Nazi War Criminal

On July 17, 1950, a man from Romania named Valerian Trifa came to the United States. Trifa was among the masses of immigrants entering the country from Eastern Europe after World War II (1939–1945). He claimed he was a displaced person who had spent time in a German concentration camp.

Soon after his arrival in the United States, Trifa was ordained as a priest of the Romanian Orthodox Church. He rose to the rank of bishop and led a church of thirty-five thousand members in Grass Lake, Michigan. In 1955, Trifa gave an opening prayer before the U.S. Senate. He became a citizen of the United States in 1957. He later became an archbishop.

But Trifa had a dark and hidden past. Dr. Charles Kremer, a Romanian-American dentist, discovered that Trifa had come to the United States. Many of Kremer's Jewish family members had been killed during a riot in Romania in 1941. Kremer sent scores of documents to the U.S. government claiming that Trifa was responsible for this crime and other crimes during World War II. Kremer pressed the government for years to prosecute Trifa.

Finally, in 1975, the U.S. Justice Department began investigating Trifa for committing war crimes. Among other charges, federal officials said that Trifa had lied on his citizenship papers. They claimed Trifa had been a Nazi sympathizer. He had been a member of the Romanian Iron

Guard, a violent pro-Nazi political movement dedicated to driving Jews out of Romania. Officials stated that in 1941 Trifa had made an anti-Semitic speech in Romania. The speech had sparked four days of attacks in which more than three hundred Jews and other Romanians were killed, including Charles Kremer's relatives. However, in order to deport (or expel) Trifa from the United States, federal officials had to prove their case.

The West German government sent the U.S. Justice Department documents tying Trifa to Nazi crimes. One intriguing piece of evidence was a postcard that Trifa had allegedly written to a high-ranking Nazi official, Heinrich Himmler—the head of the Nazi S.S. (the German combat arm of the Nazi Party)—in 1942. The postcard was signed "Viorel Trifa," which was how Trifa was known in the church. In the postcard, Trifa pledged his loyalty to the Nazi party. Nevertheless, Trifa denied writing the card.

There had to be more proof. If Trifa had written the postcard, could it still have his fingerprints on it? The West German government refused to allow the FBI to use any techniques that might destroy this historic piece of evidence. So the FBI Identification Division used a new technique—a laser—to scan the postcard for latent fingerprints. Shockingly, the laser revealed a single thumbprint that had been preserved—and had gone unnoticed—for several decades.

Because a person's fingerprints never change, and because fingerprints can remain intact on a surface for years, the FBI was able to match the fingerprint on the postcard to Trifa's fingerprints that had been taken when he became a U.S. citizen. The thumbprint on the postcard was among the most critical pieces of evidence tying Trifa to his past.

Trifa continually denied he had played a role in the attacks against Jews. When shown a photograph of himself wearing an Iron Guard uniform, he admitted to being a member of the group. He also admitted to working on an anti-Semitic newspaper and giving pro-Nazi speeches. Yet Trifa never apologized for his actions. He told a reporter in 1973, "I am not ashamed of my past at all."[1] In 1980, hoping to avoid a trial, Trifa agreed to give up his U.S. citizenship. The government, however, persisted. In the middle of a trial before an immigration judge in Detroit, Trifa voluntarily agreed to be deported. He claimed that he did so because the trial was placing a heavy financial burden on his church. When the deportation agreement was read, Charles Kremer was present in the courtroom. Trifa was deported from the United States to Portugal in 1984. He died of a heart attack in 1987 at the age of seventy-two.

Case #2: Suspected Cop Killers Nabbed After Forty-One Years

Elizabeth Bernoskie is now a grandmother in her seventies. Yet she will never forget the night of November 28, 1958—more than five decades ago. A chilly rain was falling in her hometown of Rahway, New Jersey. Her husband, police officer Charles Bernoskie, was on night patrol. The rain was so heavy that Officer Bernoskie returned home for a pair of rubber boots. "I'll be home shortly," he told his wife, who was three months pregnant with the couple's sixth child.[2] Their five older children were ages one to eight. Bernoskie sloshed out into the storm. The couple could not have known that the night would end in tragedy.

Later that evening, less than five minutes from home, Bernoskie tried to stop a robbery at a local car dealership. Two men were inside. When they heard Bernoskie rattling the door, they panicked and ran to the neighboring yard. They hid behind a shed. Bernoskie found the men, but one man took off running. Then gun shots rang out. Officer Bernoskie was shot three times. He returned fire. Despite his injuries, he stumbled to a nearby home. But it was too late. Officer Bernoskie could not be saved.

Elizabeth Bernoskie was left to raise her family alone. Police detectives worked hard to solve the murder of one of their own officers. Unfortunately, the rain had washed away most of the evidence. The gun that had fired the fatal shots was never found. The only clue that remained at the scene was a single fingerprint on a can of antifreeze. However, police could not find a match. Officer Bernoskie's murder was left unsolved for forty-one years.

In 1999, new information reopened the case. A woman named Judith Sapsa tipped off police. She turned in her brother, Robert Zarinsky, and her cousin, Ted Schiffer. Mrs. Sapsa said she remembered that on the night of Officer Bernoskie's murder, she had watched as her mother used tweezers to remove bullets from Zarinsky and Schiffer as they lay on the family's kitchen table in Linden, New Jersey. The mother, who died in 1995, had apparently been extremely protective and never confessed to police what had happened. She swore the family to secrecy. However, Mrs. Sapsa decided to come forward.

Sapsa's cousin, Ted Schiffer, was sixty-three years old at the time of his arrest. Since the murder, he had lived a quiet life in Pennsylvania. He had never been arrested or fingerprinted, so his prints never appeared in police records. When police investigated the tip, they found that Schiffer's fingerprint—taken more than forty years after the crime—matched the one lifted the night of the murder. Apparently, Schiffer and Zarinsky had been trying to steal antifreeze from the car dealership on that cold and rainy night, when Officer Bernoskie had foiled the attempt.

As in the case of Valerian Trifa, a single fingerprint tied a criminal to a crime decades later. Schiffer confessed to being at the scene on the night of the murder. He testified against the alleged shooter, Zarinsky,

The only evidence left at the crime scene of Officer Bernoskie's death was a single print on a can of antifreeze.

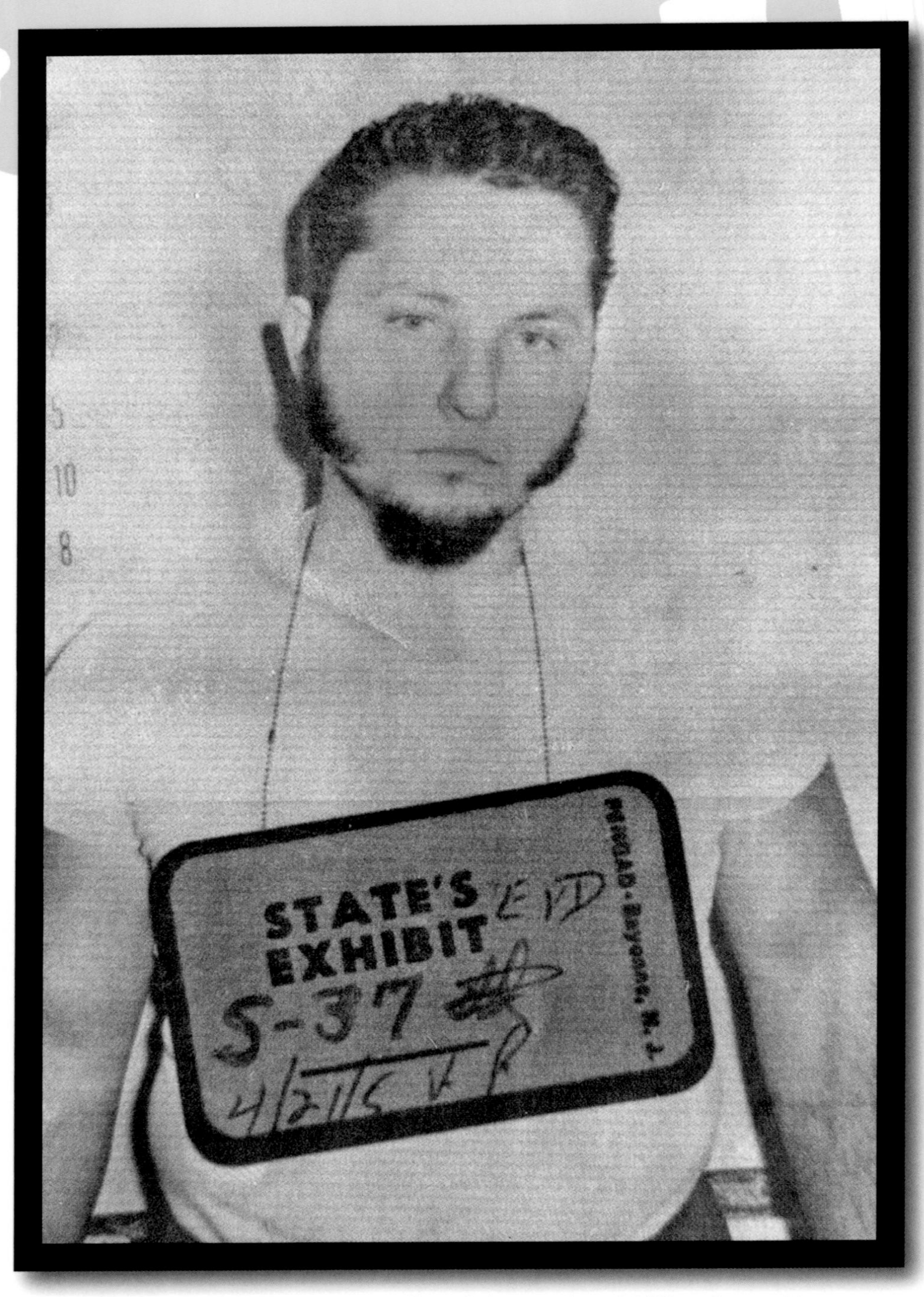

Robert Zarinsky was found not guilty of the murder of Officer Bernoskie.

who was already serving a ninety-eight-year sentence for the murder of a teenage girl. Zarinsky's rap sheet also included a long string of crimes including robbery, arson, and vandalism. Thanks to the match of a lone fingerprint, Schiffer was sent to jail for burglary. He served a three-year sentence.

The U.S. criminal justice system can be long and drawn out. In 2001, a jury in a criminal trial found Zarinsky not guilty for Officer Bernoskie's death. Some members of the jury said they believed that Zarinsky was guilty, but the only evidence against him was the testimony of Mrs. Sapsa and Mr. Schiffer. No other evidence, such as Zarinsky's fingerprint, was found at the crime scene. However, in 2003, Mrs. Bernoskie brought a civil suit for wrongful death against Zarinsky. In a civil suit, the victim or victim's family brings a case for money damages against the offender for causing physical or emotional injury. A jury found Zarinsky responsible for Officer Bernoskie's death. His widow was awarded $9.5 million. Zarinksy, however, won an appeal in 2007. Although the saga continues, Bernoskie's family is determined to see justice served.

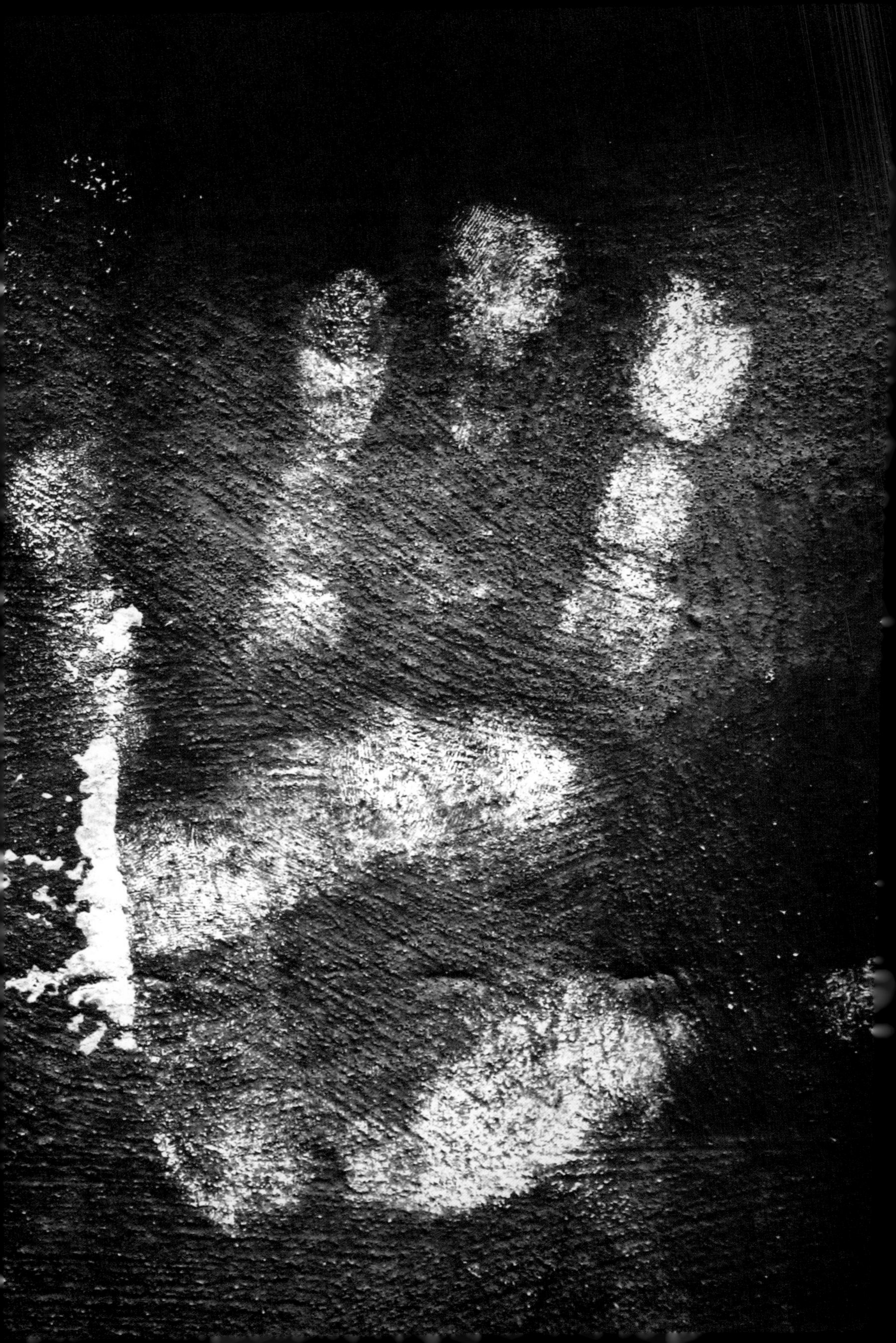

How criminals go to extremes to hide their prints

Just like criminals on television shows, bad guys in real life often think they can outwit police by hiding their fingerprints and covering their tracks. Most often they wear gloves or they try to wipe down the surfaces they touch. Some lawbreakers go to extremes to destroy their prints. For every cover-up, police try to stay one step ahead to find evidence.

In 1962, two thieves stole famous paintings from a London art gallery. The robbers thought they had outwitted police by wearing rubber gloves. However, they tossed the packaging from their gloves into a trash can. They never thought that police would search the trash and find their fingerprints on the packaging.

In another account, a gang of thieves who had carried out a series of robberies had rented an apartment. They were

Scientists can create a cast of a footprint left at a crime scene. Then they can lift the cast (right) and examine it.

very careful to wipe down counters and other surfaces to erase their fingerprints. They even loaded the dishwasher to scrub their fingerprints off their plates and glasses. The only problem: they forgot to turn on the dishwasher. Gotcha!

In 1979, a thief broke into a Burger Queen restaurant in Paris, Tennessee, and stole money from a cash box. Police dusted the place for fingerprints but couldn't find any. Strangely, a path of black footprints trailed through the office. The thief had apparently broken into the restaurant through a window. To avoid leaving his fingerprints behind, the thief had taken off his socks and had worn them on his hands. When he climbed through the window, he had stepped onto black carbon paper, which is coated in black dust. The dust stuck to the thief's bare feet. He was busted when police matched his footprints—instead of fingerprints—to the scene of the crime.

Going to Extremes

Sometimes criminals go to unbelievable extremes to "erase" their fingerprints and avoid being caught. Some have tried rubbing their fingertips with sandpaper to rub off their prints. Others resort to even more brutal methods, such as burning off their fingerprints with acid or even using surgery to slice them off. What's worse for these criminals (but good for law enforcement) is that these gruesome and painful methods usually don't work. Ridges in fingerprints run deep into the skin. Since skin is always repairing itself, fingerprints usually grow back in the same patterns. Even if the prints don't grow back completely, the scars left behind create new characteristics for an examiner to trace.

Shockingly, the first time a criminal tried to destroy his fingerprints occurred just as fingerprinting was becoming a popular crime-solving technique. In England in 1907, a suspect exited a police wagon with blood dripping from his fingers. He had used a metal tag attached to his shoelace to slice the pads of his fingertips. The man had made a desperate attempt to avoid being identified. Scotland Yard was in a frenzy. Had the man just discovered a way to bypass their new identification system? Would other crazy criminals follow his lead? Fingerprint experts waited anxiously for weeks while the suspect's fingers healed. Luckily, the ridges on the thief's fingertips grew back in the same patterns as before. His prints matched a set already on record. The man was convicted and sent to jail as a repeat criminal.

Nonetheless, criminals continue to do outrageous things to avoid arrest. Perhaps the most famous case of "fudging" fingerprints is that of John Dillinger. In the 1930s, Dillinger became known as a notorious

Since the 1930s, people have been spellbound by John Dillinger's legendary career of crime. At least seven films have been made of his life, including *Public Enemies*, a 2009 movie starring Johnny Depp as Dillinger.

bank robber and a murderer. During a crime spree that lasted several years, he robbed at least two dozen banks. With the help of his gang of fellow prisoners and girlfriends, he broke out of jail several times. During a holdup in 1934, Dillinger and his gang killed a Chicago police officer. Dillinger was sent to prison, but once again he broke free—and stole a sheriff's car. He escaped arrest so many times that he embarrassed the FBI. They assigned him the nickname "Public Enemy No. 1."

Dillinger would stop at nothing to avoid being caught. He even mutilated his own fingers! Some people claim that he tried to use acid to burn off his prints. Others say he paid a surgeon $5,000 to slice off the skin at the tips of his fingers and do some minor facial surgery.[1]

In 1934, a woman tipped off police to Dillinger's whereabouts. She told them that Dillinger would be seeing a movie at Chicago's Biograph Theater on July 22. The woman wore a red dress to signal the police. She later became known as "the lady in red." Police surrounded the theater. When they recognized Dillinger next to the lady in red, Dillinger pulled out a gun. Police shot and killed him next to the theater.

Because of Dillinger's reputation for eluding police, some people doubted that the man they had killed was in fact Public Enemy No. 1. To prove that

MYSTERY PRINTS

DID YOU KNOW that some people never develop fingerprints at all? Two very rare genetic disorders—Naegeli syndrome and Dermatopathia Pigmentosa Reticularis (DPR)—have a very unusual effect: They make a person's fingertips as smooth as glass.

they had nabbed the right man, examiners checked his fingerprints. They saw how badly he had damaged the skin at the tips of his fingers. However, some fingerprint ridges left untouched by the surgeon's scalpel (or unhurt by acid) were enough to make a match. Dillinger was definitely dead.

Botched Prints

More recently, in 1990, police in Miami arrested a suspect in a drug case. They made a gruesome discovery: The man had sliced up his fingertips and had tried to transplant pieces of skin onto other fingers. When his fingers healed, he was left with bizarrely jagged prints. Ridges ran in all directions. No match could be made using the FBI's computerized fingerprint database. Then, a fingerprint specialist had an ingenious idea. He printed photos of the suspect's butchered prints. Then he cut the photos and carefully pasted them back together like pieces of a jigsaw puzzle. The reassembled prints matched those of a man convicted in another drug case. Case solved.

Since September 11, 2001, police at border patrols have seen a new trend of people going to extremes to remove their fingerprints. This may be a response to post-9/11 efforts by the Department of Homeland Security to beef up security at border crossings. In addition to installing more security cameras and hiring more agents, Homeland Security officials have been fingerprinting every non-resident entering the United States. They run the prints through IAFIS. The prints are compared with a list of the most-wanted criminals and the FBI's terrorist watch list to see if they can find a match.

In May 2006, border police in New Mexico arrested a Jamaican man who was facing charges of handling money illegally (money laundering). They noticed that the man's fingertips were healing from surgery.

He was also limping at the time of his arrest. The man had apparently paid a surgeon to replace his fingerprints with skin from his feet! The man's painful surgery failed, and his surgeon was arrested too.

In October 2007, in Douglas, Arizona, border police arrested a twenty-five-year-old man who was caught on the Mexican border. He was trying to jump a fence into the United States. Because he had been arrested after dark, police didn't notice the man's fingertips until they arrived at the police station. When the suspect was taken for fingerprinting, agents made a grisly discovery: The man had burned the tips of his fingers with acid until they were black. However, police were still able to identify the man. He had already been convicted of an assault charge in Iowa, and he had been deported to Mexico in 2004.

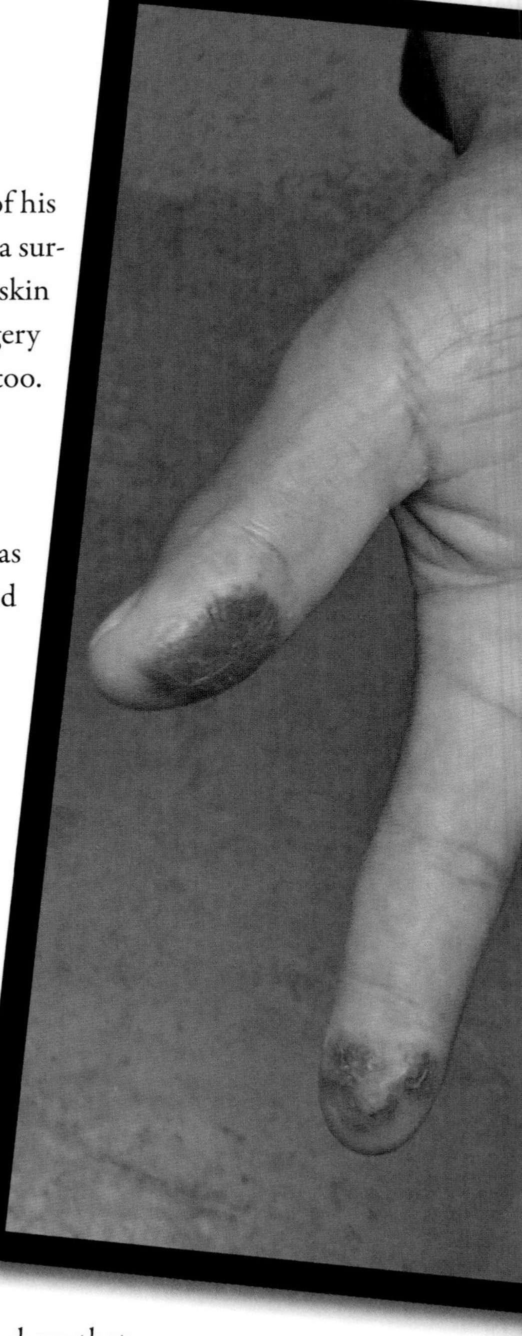

As one border official says, these cases not only show what drastic measures criminals will undergo to beat the system, they also show that fingerprinting has gained a strong reputation in the criminal world.[2] As you will see in the next chapter, however, the fingerprinting process isn't always foolproof.

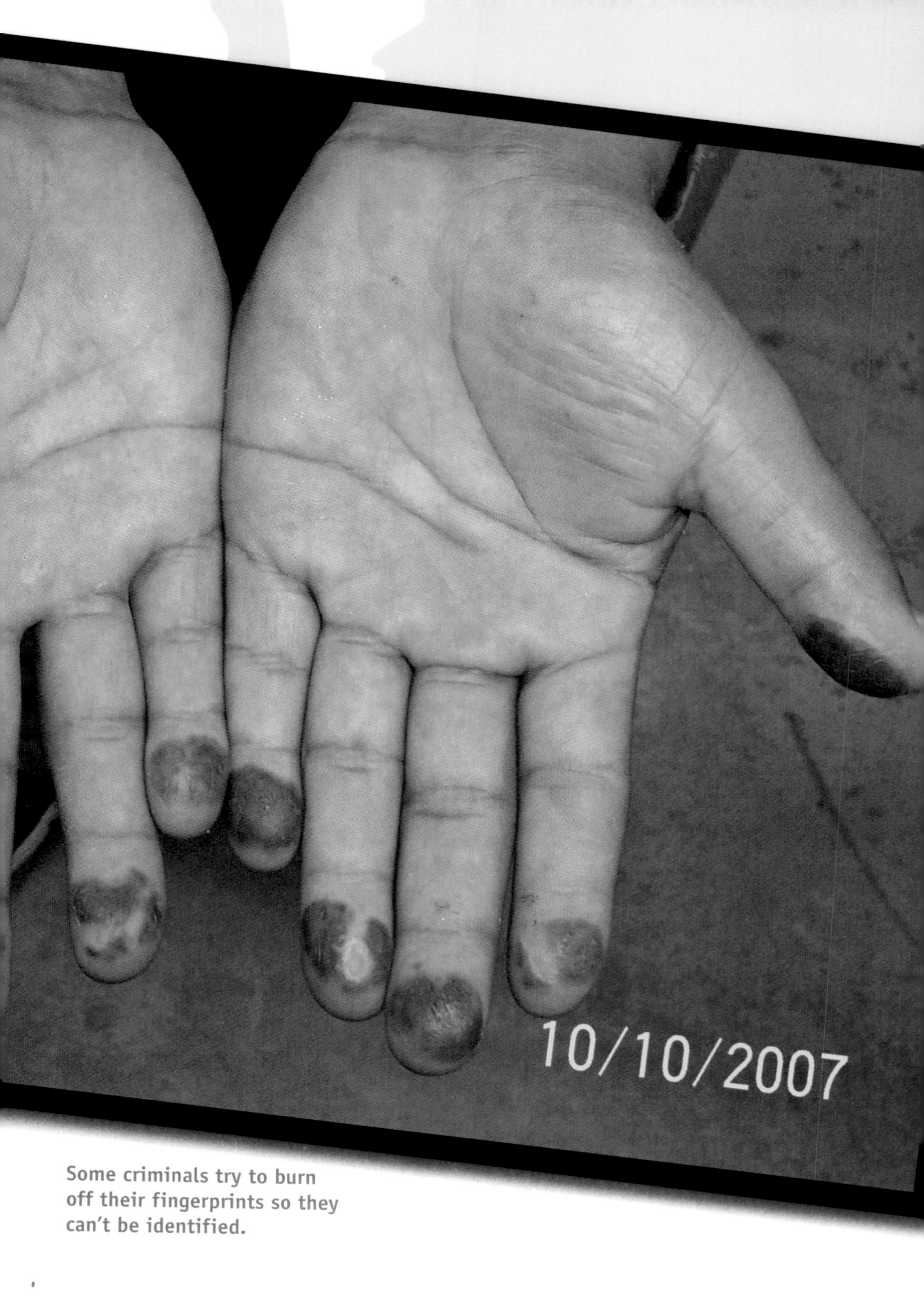

Some criminals try to burn off their fingerprints so they can't be identified.

When innocent people are sent to jail

For more than a century, fingerprinting has withstood the test of time, connecting criminals to crimes. What bolsters the success of fingerprinting is that no two people have ever been found to have exactly the same fingerprints—even identical twins. Nonetheless, over the past several years, the use of fingerprints to convict criminals has stirred up controversy. The problem, critics say, is that matching fingerprints is not an exact science. Many fingerprints that are lifted from crime scenes are smudged. Very often they are only partial prints, tiny fragments of a complete fingerprint. Even with the wide variety of techniques used to lift prints at a crime scene and the advanced technology used in crime labs to match prints, mistakes can be made. An innocent person might go to jail.

No two people have the same fingerprints, but sometimes people have very similar fingerprints. Examiners have to be very careful when comparing fingerprints to make sure a suspect isn't wrongfully accused of a crime.

Unfortunately, in a small—but growing—number of cases, this situation has actually occurred.

According to Simon Cole, associate professor of criminology (the study of crime and criminals) at the University of California, Irvine, the question isn't whether two fingerprints from different people could ever look exactly alike. The question is whether the prints of two random individuals could appear close enough to throw off a fingerprint expert. The answer—based on recent cases of mistaken identity—is yes. In one test of fingerprint examiners' skills, as many as one out of five experts misidentified fingerprint samples.[1] What's more, in a number of recent criminal cases, the wrong individual was imprisoned based on faulty fingerprint evidence. Following are three flawed-fingerprint cases in which innocent people spent time in jail for crimes they did not commit.

Friend or Foe?

One gruesome case occurred in Upper Darby, Pennsylvania, in 1997. A man named Alvin Davis was found murdered in his home. An electric box fan lay across the victim's head. Police retrieved bloody fingerprints from the fan's handle. They matched the prints to a friend of the victim, a man named Rick Jackson.

From the beginning, Jackson maintained his innocence. He claimed that the prints were not his

Firefighters help rescue people from bombed trains in Madrid, Spain, in March 2004.

and that someone had made a terrible mistake. Still, Jackson was arrested. At his trial, two local police officers who had examined the fingerprints—as well as a third examiner from out of state—testified that, without a doubt, the bloody fingerprints belonged to Jackson. The trial lasted two weeks. The jury reviewed the case for a few hours and returned the verdict: Jackson was found guilty of first-degree murder. He was sentenced to life in prison, with a chance of being released early under certain conditions.

Jackson's attorney was determined to find justice for his client. The prosecution (the legal team representing the government) had shown no motive for the murder and had presented no eyewitnesses of the crime. The only way to overturn the case would be to prove that the fingerprints on the fan were not Jackson's. Jackson's lawyer called in two former FBI fingerprint experts to analyze the prints. They both came to same conclusion: The prints found at the scene were not a match to Jackson. The differences were so obvious that one expert even thought he had been given the wrong set of prints to analyze.[2]

Jackson's case went back to court. A judge determined that the police had made a grave error. After serving two years behind bars, Jackson was set free. Alvin Davis's true killer has not yet been found.

Mistaken Madrid Bomber

During the peak of rush hour, on the morning of March 11, 2004, disaster struck. A series of bombings ripped through four commuter trains in Madrid, Spain. The bombs had been detonated in backpacks stowed on the trains. The explosions killed 191 people. As many as 2,051 others were injured by the blasts.

While searching for the terrorists who had committed these attacks, Spanish police uncovered a partial latent fingerprint on a plastic bag that contained detonators. For help with their investigation, they sent digital images of the print to the FBI. U.S. officials ran the prints through IAFIS, the FBI's computerized database. The database produced a short list of potential matches. Three FBI fingerprint experts determined that the print belonged to a man named Brandon Mayfield, a lawyer living in Oregon.

Mayfield's prints were on file because of a burglary arrest in 1984, when he was a teenager. The FBI apparently found fifteen points of comparison (or ridge characteristics) between the partial print from the bombings and Mayfield's fingerprint. U.S. officials called the match a "bingo match."[3] A fourth fingerprint examiner agreed with the match.

Mayfield was arrested as a material witness to the bombings. During a raid on Mayfield's home, the FBI took his computers, modem, safe-deposit key, papers, and copies of the Koran, a sacred Muslim text (Mayfield was a convert to Islam), as well as "Spanish documents." These later turned out to be the homework of one of Mayfield's sons.

Soon after Mayfield's arrest, Spanish authorities alerted the FBI that they had made a terrible mistake. The print actually belonged to an

Brandon Mayfield was innocent, but he was arrested for the Madrid bombings based on fingerprint evidence.

Algerian man named Ouhnane Daoud. Mayfield had absolutely no ties to the bombings. In fact, he hadn't left the United States in ten years. He was released after spending two weeks in jail. All of his property was returned to him. He described his time in jail as "humiliating" and "embarrassing."[4] When other inmates learned about his suspected terrorist ties, he had feared for his safety.

Mayfield later sued the U.S. Justice Department for their serious blunder. In November 2006, he was awarded a $2 million settlement. He also received an apology from the Justice Department and the FBI as well as an agreement that the FBI would destroy any conversations they had recorded from his home and office during the investigation.

Loose-fitting Genes

On May 30, 1997, after a struggle with an unknown attacker, Boston police officer Sergeant Gregory Gallagher was shot with his own gun in the backyard of a house. The attacker also fired a shot at a witness watching from a second-story window. Running from the scene, the shooter left behind a baseball cap. Then he forced his way into a nearby home and drank water from a glass mug. He fled that home as well, leaving behind the gun and a white sweatshirt that he had worn.

About two weeks later, the injured police officer looked at mug shots of possible suspects. He picked a man named Stephan Cowans as the shooter. He later chose Cowans out of a lineup, a group of people lined up by police for identification by witnesses to a crime. The witness from the upstairs window also selected Cowans from a lineup. Yet the family who lived in the house that the attacker had entered did not identify Cowans.

Nevertheless, at the trial, the jury relied on the testimony of Sergeant Gallagher and that of the upstairs neighbor. Jurors also focused on a latent fingerprint that was found on the glass that the attacker had used.

Stephan Cowans was wrongfully imprisoned based on faulty fingerprint evidence. He was released after serving five and a half years in prison.

Fingerprint experts claimed that the fingerprint belonged to Cowans. He was convicted on numerous counts, including assault and battery of a police officer, home invasion, and battery by means of a dangerous weapon. He was sentenced to thirty to forty-five years in prison.

On May 22, 2003, new evidence surfaced in the case. At the request of Cowans's lawyer, the Suffolk Superior Court issued a release of the key pieces of evidence: the glass mug, swabs taken from the mug, the baseball cap, and the sweatshirt. All of the evidence was tested for DNA, the molecular blueprint in cells that makes each person unique. Stephan Cowans's DNA did not match the DNA on these items. In addition, a re-examination of the fingerprint found on the drinking glass proved that it did not belong to Cowans. He could not have been the attacker.

On January 23, 2004, Stephan Cowans walked out of prison a free man. He had served five and a half years for a crime he did not commit. The real attacker is still on the loose.

Reasonable Doubt?

Today, many people are becoming skeptical about the accuracy of fingerprint analysis. Cases like these bring several flaws to the forefront. First, questions arise as to who can be considered a fingerprint expert. All fingerprint examiners go through training, which can take several months. An organization called the International Association for Identification gives a certifying exam to fingerprint examiners. However, many crime labs—including the FBI lab—do not require certification for officers to identify fingerprints. In Rick Jackson's case, the prosecution's out-of-state expert was certified, and he still made a terrible mistake. In addition, judges do not require that fingerprint examiners who testify in court be certified. The bottom line, critics say, is that fingerprint analysis is based on human judgment, and all humans make mistakes.

Another major problem with fingerprint analysis, according to Jennifer L. Mnookin, a professor at the UCLA School of Law, is that it is not an exact science.[5] In court, a fingerprint expert can testify that a match is certain. Yet that claim cannot be proven. Studies have never been completed to demonstrate how often two random people could have similar fingerprints. After more than a century of fingerprint analysis, many questions still remain unanswered. How often do similar fingerprints confuse examiners? What about partial prints? Can small fragments of two different people's prints be the same? We simply don't know.

In addition, fingerprint examiners might have knowledge of a case that could lead to bias or taint their assumptions. It makes one wonder: How often do such judgment calls creep into fingerprint analysis?

What's more, in the United States, there are no agreed-upon standards as to what is considered a fingerprint match. Other countries have devised systems to determine how many points of similarity in ridge patterns are required to make a match. In Italy, the number is sixteen or seventeen points. In Brazil, the number is thirty. In Australia, you need twelve points to make a match. In the United States, fingerprints have been declared a match with as few as seven or eight points. The number may vary from precinct to precinct, or between any two fingerprint examiners.[6]

According to criminologist Simon Cole, in the future, fingerprinting may be pushed aside by a much more scientific and sophisticated identification instrument—DNA. Introduced in the 1980s, DNA profiling has revolutionized forensic science. Unlike fingerprint comparison, DNA profiling developed over the past few decades through extensive biological research at top-notch academic centers. Every person who is not an identical twin has unique DNA. According to the FBI, when DNA evidence is presented at trial, their experts can testify with

99 percent certainty that a specific individual—and no other person in the country—is the source of the DNA.[7] As of now, a good deal of fingerprint evidence cannot be presented with the same degree of certainty.

A person's DNA is the same in every cell of the body that has a nucleus (such as skin, muscle, and nerve cells). A lab needs only thirty to fifty microscopic cells to make a match. Today's highly sensitive equipment may even be able to make a match with as few as six cells. However, the admissibility in court of such small samples has not been established.

DNA can be collected in minute traces—from blood, saliva, sweat, hair, and body tissues. It can even be lifted from skin cells left in a fingerprint. When a person is tied to a crime through DNA, there are reliable statistics—and a significant amount of scientific data—to back up that claim. In addition, even in small amounts, DNA has a set structure. It can be digitized and analyzed on computers. Fingerprints taken from a crime scene can be much fuzzier. A smudged print, for

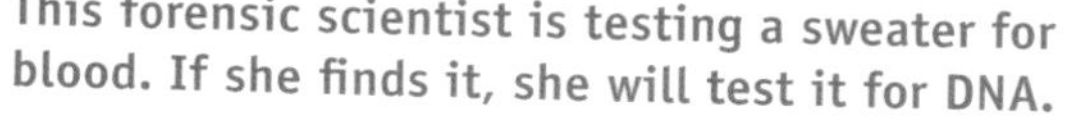
This forensic scientist is testing a sweater for blood. If she finds it, she will test it for DNA.

example, may reveal a tiny segment of a ridge pattern, with very few points of comparison. A clear copy of the same print, meanwhile, will have many more points of comparison. Other factors play a role in the quality of a fingerprint, such as the surface that the print was found on (for example, paper or glass) or the pressure of the fingers that created the print.

Fingerprinting, as Cole says, seems "so last century." Think about the history of criminal identification. About a hundred years ago, fingerprinting displaced the body-measurement system devised by Alphonse Bertillon. At the time the world was advancing rapidly, becoming more technological and scientific. In the twenty-first century, as DNA analysis becomes more mainstream, is it possible that fingerprinting will be phased out?

Everybody Makes Mistakes

For the most part, individuals who work in forensic science—police, crime lab investigators, and many legal experts—don't believe that fingerprint analysis will be left in the dust. In fact, fingerprint technology is improving rapidly and becoming more precise. Experts have seen time and again how criminals can be identified when they leave their fingerprints at the scene of a crime. They acknowledge that mistakes may occur, but they are rare.

Nevertheless, when people's lives are at stake, who wants to take a chance? In February 2009, the National Academy of Sciences released a report by a panel of forensic experts. They found that many of the techniques used in crime labs have major problems. One significant claim is that unlike DNA, fingerprinting has never undergone extensive scientific research. Instead of being studied in a scientific lab, much of the research in fingerprinting has been conducted in crime labs or is being argued by legal experts in courtrooms.

To make the process more accurate and to prevent mistakes in the future, many people are now pushing for further study of fingerprint analysis and improvements in the field. Cases of mistaken identity—which can ruin innocent lives while keeping criminals on the street—will hopefully be prevented. Perhaps if better guidelines had been in place, people like Jackson, Mayfield, and Cowans would never have been sent to jail in the first place.

FINE-TUNING FINGERPRINTS

MANY EFFORTS are under way to improve the accuracy of fingerprint analysis. Here are a few examples:

- Scientists are creating computer models to determine how often two random fingerprints might look the same. This will help legal experts and juries understand the likelihood of a match.
- Studies are being developed to determine how often outside information influences decisions in fingerprint identification and what can be done in these cases to prevent bias.
- New technology is being developed to make fingerprinting more accurate and more sensitive.
- Suggested guidelines for fingerprint examiners:
  - improved training
  - clear guidelines regarding certification
  - more testing of examiners' skills
  - constant review of match results to help eliminate mistakes and possible bias.

WANTED: FINGERPRINT EXAMINER

JOB TITLE: CRIME SCENE TECHNICIAN

Description: Detect, collect, and preserve physical evidence (including fingerprints) found at crime scenes; process and analyze fingerprints; photograph evidence; prepare evidence for submission to labs; maintain fingerprint records; conduct latent print examinations using AFIS; prepare crime scene reports for presentation in court

Education: Minimum of Associate Degree in forensic science, biology, chemistry, criminal justice or related field; experience in crime scene investigation, forensics, or related criminal justice work involving required skills, knowledge, and abilities

Salary range: $30,000–$49,000 (varies by experience and department)

JOB TITLE: FINGERPRINT TECHNICIAN

Description: Take and process fingerprints and palm prints and photographs of prisoners; use Live Scan and manual equipment to collect fingerprints and palm prints; transmit images through computer systems; identify basic ten prints; compare and classify physical details of fingerprints; maintain records

Education: Completion of formal or college-level course in fingerprint identification; at least six months in law enforcement in which duties include taking, classifying, and comparing fingerprints

Salary range: $44,000–$53,000 (varies by experience and department)

JOB TITLE: LATENT PRINT EXAMINER

Description: Process fingerprint evidence collected at a crime scene or from an investigative agency (police, FBI, etc.); conduct latent print comparisons to determine identities for use in police investigations; operate computerized database searches; obtain prints from deceased people; testify in court

Education: College degree (B.S. in biology or chemistry preferred)
To become certified (recommended, but not required): College degree; minimum two years of full-time experience as a latent print examiner; completion of certification exam

Average Salary: $44,000–$55,000 (may vary depending upon region, years of experience, and type of agency—local, state, or federal)

JOB TITLE: LATENT PRINT SUPERVISOR

Description: Supervise, assign, and evaluate work of technical personnel involved in latent print identification; train staff and police in latest methods and practices in fingerprint and related criminal identification work and in new laws, procedures, and policies in the field; train employees to use AFIS; compile and evaluate statistics regarding latent prints; provide expert witness testimony in court

Education: Minimum three years as latent print examiner (depending on department)

Average salary: $55,000–$88,000 (may vary depending upon region, years of experience, and type of agency—local, state, or federal)

7 INSTANT ID

The future of fingerprinting

One hundred years ago, when fingerprinting was emerging as a new crime-solving technique, no one could have foreseen how far-reaching fingerprint analysis would be today. What's more, people who work in the field of personal identification see little evidence of fingerprinting being phased out or replaced. In fact, fingerprinting appears to be more widespread than ever.

Picture this scenario. You're standing at the entrance to Disney's Magic Kingdom. The line seems to go on forever. You can't wait to buy your ticket and head over to the rides in Tomorrowland. As you enter the park, the attendant asks you to scan your fingerprints. Are you busted? What's going on?

Since 2006, visitors at Disney World's four Orlando theme parks have been asked to scan their fingerprints at the entrance. According to park officials, this measure allows them to protect against ticket fraud. If you buy a multi-day pass, you are the only one who can use it. You are not permitted to re-sell your multi-day ticket (which lowers the price of a daily pass) to make a profit. Fingerprints are an instant way to prove that you are *you*.

The Disney scenario is a stark reminder of how far fingerprint technology has come. For decades, police relied on ink pads and fingerprint cards to nab criminals. They slogged through hundreds—or thousands—of fingerprint cards trying to make a match. Today, all you have to do is scan your fingerprint and you're in the system.

Keeping up with technology, in 2007 the FBI embarked on a new project called Next Generation Identification. It is a $1 billion plan to build the world's largest computer database of people's physical characteristics. The database relies on biometrics, the automated recognition of people based on distinctive traits and behaviors. The database will include digital images of fingerprints, faces, and palm prints, as well as the patterns in irises (the colored part of the eye), face-shape data, scars, and perhaps even data about the different ways people walk and talk. For the FBI, the new computerized system will be broader, faster, and more accurate than ever before. The database is expected to be fully operational by 2013.

You've probably seen biometrics in action in spy movies and sci-fi thrillers like *Star Trek*. What tourists at Disney World—and all of the rest of us—are witnessing today is the introduction of biometrics in everyday life. These systems are becoming more and more common in routine tasks. Today, to log on to certain laptop computers, mobile phones, ATMs, and other technology, you must first scan your fingerprint. Government agencies use fingerprints to check the backgrounds of job applicants.

Some high school cafeterias are trying out a cashless payment system in which students scan their fingerprints to buy lunch. School libraries are using fingerprints to check out books. Even supermarkets are testing fingerprint scanners as a quick way for people to pay for groceries. Banks across the United States are using fingerprint scans to cut down on check fraud. The theory is that thieves can forge a written signature on a check, but they can't forge a fingerprint.

As you have seen, fingerprints have proven to be reliable sources of identification because they are, as far as we know, unique to each person, and because they don't change over time. Being able to scan your fingerprints might also make life a bit easier: You won't

Students have their fingerprints scanned in a cafeteria. The fingerprint scan is linked to the student's account, and automatically deducts the price of their lunch.

have to remember to carry ID cards with you and you won't have to memorize multiple passwords or PINs.

Scientists, such as Anil K. Jain, a professor of computer science and engineering at Michigan State University, are working on programs to make fingerprinting technology more accurate. One challenge that Dr. Jain faces is designing biometric systems that can't be fooled. Say, for example, that someone uses a biometric system to protect a safe full of jewels. The safe has a scanner that recognizes the owner's fingerprint. A crafty thief might be able to lift the owner's print, make a plastic copy of it, and break into the safe. Researchers are now developing systems containing sensors that detect body heat and other signs of life. In addition, Jain notes that systems that recognize multiple traits (for example, ten prints instead of one, or faces in addition to fingerprints) tend to be more accurate and reliable.

As of January 18, 2009, visitors entering the United States at border crossings and other ports of entry must now have all ten of their fingerprints scanned. (Originally, when the program debuted in 2004, only two fingers were scanned.) This is part of US-VISIT (U.S. Visitor and

Foreign visitors to the United States must now have all ten of their fingerprints scanned.

Immigrant Status Indicator Technology), a program run through the Department of Homeland Security. Photographs and digital prints are collected and matched against a watch list of known criminals and suspected terrorists to help ensure that these individuals do not try to enter the country. The US-VISIT program has already scanned the prints of more than 100 million visitors.

Privacy Matters

Such uses of fingerprint technology—from border crossings to theme park entries to school lunch lines—have people who want to protect privacy on high alert. They want to know: Who will have access to your prints? What does your fingerprint tell someone about who you are, where you have been, or how you spend your time and money? The question for everyone else becomes: At what point does a process that enhances security become an invasion of privacy? Are you willing to give up some privacy in order to be safe? Will the government or a private company be able to track you down wherever you are? Will people be under constant surveillance?

On the flip side, is all the clamor about fingerprints and privacy just a matter of getting used to new technology, like wireless Internet or text messaging? Has fingerprint technology gone too far—or not far enough? What do *you* think?

I live with my family in a very quiet, pleasant, and friendly suburb of New York City. During the day, our front door is usually open for our friends to come and go. We always feel safe and secure. Unless we're reading the newspaper or watching TV, crime doesn't usually cross our minds.

Suddenly, while I was writing this book, that safety bubble burst. On June 30, 2009, my close friend and neighbor Rachelle called to say that her house had been robbed. The thief had broken in through a window in broad daylight when no one was home. He had stolen two laptop computers, jewelry, watches, and an iPod.

Rachelle was reassured by the police officers who came to investigate. "The police were in my house for three hours searching for fingerprints," she said. "They were very thorough." ("Fingerprints!" I thought. "This could get exciting.")

Yet the crafty thief was one step ahead of police. Two other houses nearby were broken into within three weeks. We soon learned from police that these robberies were part of a string of more than *forty* break-ins in our town, plus others in surrounding neighborhoods—all within a four-month period. Finally, after a few weeks, police made a break in the case. Guess what? It all hinged on a fingerprint! Here's what happened: On July 6, the thief had broken into another home a few houses away from mine. He had stolen two handguns, a digital camera, computers, and other property. Apparently, to get into the house, the thief had grasped the top of a screen door with his bare hands and then kicked in the door to the house.

Later that day, a savvy police detective dusted the top rim of the screen door for fingerprints. He discovered and lifted a print. When police ran the print through IAFIS, they found a match! The fingerprint belonged to a man named Peter Soja. His prints were on record because he had already served time in jail two times, once for burglary and once for drug possession. Now the thief had a name and a face. The warrant for his arrest included armed burglary, theft, and gun possession. Crime Stoppers offered a $1,000 reward for information leading to his arrest. Unless this guy was a master of disguise, we felt certain he would be caught soon.

Soja managed to elude police for another week. At long last, on July 14, I received an e-mail from my friend Rachelle that read, "Thief caught!!!" Police had recognized Soja walking on the street of a nearby town. He was carrying a backpack full of stolen goods. Busted!

Soja confessed to many of the robberies and is now spending time in jail while he awaits sentencing.

"We were so happy to see the system working," Rachelle said. She even got some of her jewelry back. As I breathed a sigh of relief, I now had solid proof that fingerprinting does solve crimes.

As Teaneck Police Officer James Deanni told me, "Eventually these guys mess up. Their luck only lasts so long."[1]

CHAPTER NOTES

CHAPTER 1. THE WILD WILL WEST STORY

1. Colin Beavan, *Fingerprints* (New York: Hyperion, 2001), p. 80.
2. Joe Nickell and John F. Fischer, *Crime Science: Methods of Forensic Detection* (Lexington: The University Press of Kentucky, 1999), p. 115.
3. Edward P. Richards, "Phenotype v. Genotype: Why Identical Twins Have Different Fingerprints," n.d., <http://www.forensic-evidence.com/site/ID/ID_Twins.html> (November 19, 2009).
4. Peter H. Warman and A. Roland Ennos, "Fingerprints are unlikely to increase friction of primate fingerpads," *The Journal of Experimental Biology*, vol. 212, June 12, 2009, pp. 2016–2022.
5. Elizabeth Landau, "Fingerprint study offers inspiration for robotics research," February 3, 2009, <http://edition.cnn.com/2009/HEALTH/02/03/fingerprints.study/index.html> (November 17, 2009).
6. Christopher J. Lennard, "Fingerprint Patterns," *The Thin Blue Line Information Section*, n.d., <http://www.policensw.com/info/fingerprints/finger07.html >(November 30, 2009).
7. David Fisher, *Hard Evidence* (New York: Dell Publishing, 1996), p. 174.

CHAPTER 2. ON THE RECORD

1. Henry Faulds, *Nature,* vol.xxii, October 28, 1880, p. 605.
2. Illinois Supreme Court, People v. Jennings, 252 Ill. 534, 96 N.E. 1077 (1911); Mark A. Acree, "People v. Jennings: A Significant Case in American Fingerprint History," n.d., <http://www.scafo.org/library/140401.html> (August 11, 2009).

3. Federal Bureau of Investigation, "Integrated Automated Fingerprint Identification System," March, 13, 2008, <http://www.fbi.gov/hq/cjisd/iafis.htm> (November 30, 2009).
4. Barbara Gardner Conklin, Robert Gardner, and Dennis Shortelle, *Encyclopedia of Forensic Science* (Santa Barbara, Calif.: Greenwood Press, 2002), p. 109.
5. Ellen Nakashima, "FBI Prepares Vast Database of Biometrics; $1 Billion Project to Include Images of Irises and Faces," *The Washington Post*, December 22, 2007, p. A1.

CHAPTER 3. THE HUNT

1. Personal interview with Lyla Thompson, December 2, 2009.
2. David Fisher, *Hard Evidence* (New York: Dell Publishing, 1996), p. 169.

CHAPTER 4. YOU CAN RUN, BUT YOU CAN'T HIDE

1. Ari L. Goldman, "Valerian Trifa, an Archbishop with a Fascist Past, Dies at 72," *The New York Times*, January 29, 1987, p. B6.
2. "The Murder of Officer Bernoskie" (transcript), *60 Minutes II*, CBS News, March 27, 2002.

CHAPTER 5. FUDGING FINGERPRINTS

1. David Fisher, *Hard Evidence* (New York: Dell Publishing, 1996), p. 175.
2. Mimi Hall, "Criminals Go to Extremes to Hide Identities," *USA Today*, November, 6, 2007, <http://www.usatoday.com/news/nation/2007-11-06-criminal-extreme_N.htm> (July 2, 2008).

CHAPTER 6: FINGERPRINT FLAWS

1. Simon Cole, "The Myth of Fingerprints," *The New York Times*, May 13, 2001, <http://www.nytimes.com/2001/05/13/magazine/the-way-we-live-now-5-13-01-the-myth-of-fingerprints.html> (March 24, 2009).
2. Peter Moser, "Can Forensic Evidence Be Disputed?" April 24, 2008, <http://forensicscience.suite101.com> (July 15, 2009).
3. Jennifer L. Mnookin, "The Achilles' Heel of Fingerprints," *The Washington Post*, May 29, 2004, p. A27.
4. The Associated Press, "FBI Apologizes to Lawyer in Bombing Case," May 25, 2004, <http://www.msnbc.msn.com/id/5053007/> (July 10, 2009).
5. Jennifer L. Mnookin, "Fingerprints: Not a Gold Standard," *Issues in Science and Technology* (University of Texas at Dallas), October 9, 2003, <http:www.issues.org/20.1/mnookin.html> (December 3, 2009).
6. Nina Eaglin, "Fingerprints: Infallible Evidence?" (transcript), *60 Minutes*, CBS News, June 6, 2004.
7. Bruce Budowle, Ranajit Chakaborty, George Carmody, and Keith L. Monson, "Source Attribution of a Forensic DNA Profile," *Journal of Forensic Science Communication*, vol. 2, no. 3, July 2000, <www.fbi.gov/hq/lab/fsc/backissue/july2000/index> (November 26, 2009).

AFTERWORD: THE SYSTEM AT WORK

1. Personal interview with Police Officer James Deanni, July 16, 2009.

GLOSSARY

arch—A fingerprint pattern that slopes upward and downward like a hill.

dactylography—The scientific study of fingerprints for the purpose of identification.

dactyloscopy—The technique of taking someone's fingerprints.

fingerprint—The pattern of ridges at the tip of a finger.

friction—The force that resists motion between two objects.

latent fingerprint—A fingerprint that is not readily visible.

loop—A fingerprint pattern that begins on one side of a fingertip, curves around, and exits on the other side.

minutiae—Ridge details used to compare fingerprints.

patent fingerprint—A fingerprint that is visible to the naked eye.

plastic fingerprint—A 3-D molded impression of a fingerprint found in soft materials such as soap, paint, or wet cement.

ridge—A raised line of skin that forms a pattern at the tip of a finger.

whorl—A spiral or circular fingerprint pattern.

FURTHER READING

BOOKS

Beres, D.B., and Anna Prokos. *Crime Scene: True-Life Forensic Files: Dusting and DNA*. New York: Scholastic Inc., 2008.

Hueske, Edward. *Firearms and Fingerprints.* New York: Facts On File, Inc., 2008

Innes, Brian. *Fingerprints and Impressions.* Armonk, N.Y.: Sharpe Focus, 2008.

Yancey, Diane. *Murder*. San Diego, Calif.: Lucent Books, 2006.

Yount, Lisa. *Forensic Science: From Fibers to Fingerprints*. New York: Chelsea House Publishers, 2006.

INTERNET ADDRESSES

National Institute of Standards and Technology. "Police Station: Suspects' Prints." January 1, 2001.
<http://www.nist.gov/public_affairs/licweb/suspect.htm>

PBS Kids. "DragonflyTV." 2006.
<http://pbskids.org/dragonflytv/show/forensics.html?video=forensics>

The Montreal Science Centre. "Interactive File—Autopsy of a Murder."
<http://www.centredessciencesdemontreal.com/autopsy/flash.htm>

Index

G

H

I

J